Closing the Me-You Gap

Vickie Gray

Also by Vickie Gray:

Creating Time

Another book in the Simple Rules And Tools Series

ISBN: 147765464X
ISBN-13: 978-1477654644

For Paul
For giving me the very best reason to close the me-you gap

CONTENTS

ACKNOWLEDGMENTS

Jim and Michele McCarthy are the brilliant minds behind BootCamp, the most innovative group behavioral laboratory for the discovery of successful behaviours of self-organized teams I know of. The results of that experiment, the Core Commitments and Protocols (The Core), are taught and used worldwide, in face-to-face and virtual teams, families, and communities. Jim and Michele have become beloved friends and mentors for Paul and me. They inspire us with their courage, compassion and wisdom, and I value the ongoing opportunity to continue to work and play with them.

The participants of BootCamps Paul and I have instructed continue to teach and inspire me. Many of them are part of the social media extension of BootCamp on Facebook called The Booted. With Jim and Michele's help, the Booted is a global community of people who are experimenting with closing the gap online using the Core Commitments and Protocols. The openhearted courage and generosity of spirit I find there give me hope.

My Twitter friends help me stay fresh with new learning, new ideas and new connections. They teach me lessons about how to close the gap with strangers and the rewards of trust and sharing.

I would particularly like to thank those brave souls who agreed to read parts of this book before the final polish was applied: Gitte Klitgaard Hansen, Pam Fox Rollin, Staffan Noteberg, Ted Young, Sameer and Meghana Bendre, Steve Rogalsky, Donald Gray, Olaf Lewitz, Örn Haraldsson, Torbjörn Gyllebring, Sylvia Taylor, Andrea Lohnes, Catherine Gray, Eric Mignot, Dan Mezick, Heather Dennis, Oana Juncu, Stephanie Beaton, Bernard Vander Beken, Christophe Thibaut, and Steve Holyer. Some of you gave me ideas that have made a significant difference to this book. Thank you for sharing your thoughts and support with me. And thank you to everyone who helped me choose the cover art. Even better than getting your vote was to see inside each of you a little as you told me why you chose your favourite.

My coach, Karen Cappello helps me remember that ease, joy and fun are much more interesting than effort, criticism and struggle. She is a magnificent executive coach.

Finally, Paul Reeves taught me that there is a really good reason to close the me-you gap: there's love, fun, joy and wisdom on the other side. And really good coffee. He has been my Constant Reader, a tireless and cheerful supporter, and fearless with the editor's red pen.

INTRODUCTION

Our distrust is very expensive.
- Ralph Waldo Emerson

My first book, Creating Time, shares the learning of hundreds of teams, families, and pairs, who use the Core Commitments and Protocols (the Core) for designing and producing products and delivering services, making decisions, meeting, innovating, sharing ideas, and iterating to improve. Along the way readers discover that by using the Core, they create a kind of time machine.

Since I wrote that book, and spoke with people who used it with their teams, I realized we need another conversation as well, one that addresses something even more fundamental: every team is a web of two-person connections. Two people at a time, we have to trust one another for the whole team to thrive.

Every moment, each of us makes a decision about how much to trust the person in front of us. Every decision, every action, every conflict involves me (and everyone is a "me") choosing how vulnerable I will be with you (and everyone is also a "you").

Every moment, I decide whether or not I will share my ideas with you, how much support I will give you, whether or not I will try to reach resolution if we disagree, or how much help I will show you I need. Teams are continually changing webs of me sharing myself with you, and you with him, and him with her, and her with me, and every other combination possible.

The result of those interactions is greater than the sum of its parts. When we close those gaps, the sum looks like agility, effectiveness, engagement, cooperation, creativity and innovation. When we let the gaps drift open, the sum show up as waste, heaviness of process, need for certainty and control, lack of creativity and engagement and "every man for himself."

In Closing The Me-You Gap, I share some ideas about this fundamental particle of teamwork - you and me - and how we can use the Core Commitments and Protocols to make that fundamental particle as strong, safe, free, accountable and intentional as possible.

I'm writing from experience.

I have had connections that were delightful, innovative, meaningful, loyal, loving, fun and fascinating. I've also had ones that made me want to run away. Perhaps you've had connections like these, too, or someone has told you about theirs.

We each trust differently. And we each have different ways we approach one another – some quite openly, some cautiously, lots somewhere in between depending on the time, the place, and the people. But most of us have known times when lack of trust, either in others, or ourselves, got in the way of moving forward.

The roadblock we all face is that each of us is a "me" to ourselves. Each of us is also a "you" to everyone else. I can't know what it's like to be you. Nor can you know what it's like to be me.

When I try to get closer to you, I bump up against the unknown and the unknowable. There's a gap between you and me that's filled with uncertainty. Uncertainty makes me afraid, and that fear makes me hold back. Even as I reach toward you for connection, I hesitate, sometimes a lot, sometimes just a little, protecting myself from the unknown.

My hesitation affects my personal and work relationships, my sense of belonging in the world, and my confidence to take action on what I believe in. It also affects you; you see my hesitation and react.

We've all seen the effect of that hesitation when we try to work together. We don't ask for help when we really need it. We avoid conflict and hurting others feelings. We don't explain our behaviour when we're feeling strongly about something. We make assumptions instead of asking about intent. And so much more.

When we hold back from each other like this, work gets harder. It takes more time to get anything done. The products we make and the services we deliver don't live up to their potential. We look for certainty in structure and process. And we may even begin to lose enthusiasm for the work itself.

Let's say you and I want to get some work done, perhaps for our boss, for our community or ourselves. We each bring some passion, knowledge, skills and interest to solving a problem that matters to us both.

But we've never met before and don't know each other. We've never talked about the projects we've worked on, our favourite books, what kind of coffee we like, who we love, or what keeps us up at night.

Do you trust me?

Perhaps trust is easy for you. But what if it isn't for me? Or what if it's easy for me, and hard for you? Just because one of us trusts easily doesn't mean the gap is closed. The other person still has a distance to travel. As the song goes, "it takes two to tango."

We all use the gap, mostly unconsciously, every moment we're together. It's a tool in our arsenal of getting through life in one piece. By the time we're adults, we are masters at managing the gap.

We start in childhood, lying to our parents about who knocked over the lamp, who took the good scissors, and where we were on Saturday night. Then we take those years of practice unconsciously into our adult workplaces, neighbourhoods and families.

We use it with the boss, the policeman, and the new guy down the hall. We let it narrow, a little or a lot, for our families, partners, old friends, mentors, and people who have shared difficult times with us. Sometimes, it's with those very people that we *don't* close the gap, because we have evidence that we will be safer if we keep the gap wide.

Most of us let it close a little when we've had a chance to see each other in action. Circumstances can sometimes arise that force uncomfortable truths to come out, or throw us together without our choosing. But until those random circumstances occur, we wait and watch.

We "sniff out" the new boss, waiting to see if he does what he says, makes good decisions, and supports us. We observe each other in meetings to see what patterns of behaviour emerge. We gossip about the new intern and gather data about who he is from each other, but rarely directly from him. We watch the new neighbors from between the curtains until we think we know who they are.

This makes for a lot of lonely, vigilant, waiting and watching. And the more people you have, the more gaps there are. The gaps between us can create gridlock in our team and organizational communication that slows us down.

Take a common project at work, for example, and imagine for a minute you're the boss. You know you need a group of people to work on something your organization has never done before. That means you've got to bring together people who may never have worked together. You want your smartest people, your rock stars, on this team.

You pick three people: Joan, Bob and me.

You know that since we all work in different parts of the organization, we've never met before. So you arrange a project kickoff meeting, and you ask us all to introduce ourselves and tell each other a little about who we are and what we bring to the project.

I tell Bob and Joan about the work I've done with the company in the past, and I mention my interest in greyhound rescue. They tell me about their careers and hobbies. Joan and Bob also exchange some information with each other. Each of us is holding ourselves back, staying safe, reading body language, not giving anything away, trying to impress, trying to be polite, sniffing the air. Right now, there are **three** me-you gaps on this **team of three** people.

Me-Bob
Me-Joan
Bob-Joan

We start working together and after a couple of weeks of dancing around each other, having a few disagreements and misunderstandings, a few laughs, and building a "story" about each other in our heads, we get to the usual first milestone in the project. Typically, we're behind schedule, over budget, confused and frustrated. Each of us thinks that if we just had another person on the team, we could move forward.

We appeal to you – our boss - for more money, people and time. Since the company has never done this kind of project before, and you're frankly too busy to really be involved, you don't know whether or not we're right. And, after all, we're the best you've got. You believe you have no other choice.

So, skeptically, you answer our prayers and give us the person we asked for - Yves. We're thrilled and relieved, and we bring Yves up to speed on the project to date.

We're spending a lot of time in meetings, and we don't all see the project the same way. We're working a lot of hours and the amount of work seems to be increasing, as we get further behind. Soon enough, we all realize this project is much bigger and more complex than anyone imagined. Secretly, we're each blaming each other for the team's problems. The me-you gaps have increased to **six** on our **team of four**:

Me-Bob
Me-Joan
Me-Yves
Bob-Joan
Bob-Yves
Joan-Yves

We're getting really worried, so we ask you again for more people, money and time. You're starting to get worried, too. Giving us one more person last time didn't seem to help, but again, you give us the best person you have – Anne - someone we hope will solve all our problems. We now have a **team of five** and the me-you gaps have grown to **ten**:

Me-Bob
Me-Joan
Me-Yves
Me-Anne
Bob-Joan

Bob-Yves
Bob-Anne
Joan-Yves
Joan-Anne
Yves-Anne

You can see where this is going.

The problem is, boss, the more gaps you have, the more time it takes the individuals to understand each other and make themselves understood, and the more often you have to intervene and facilitate conversations when that understanding fails.

As the project begins to drag, you start to push the team harder to deliver. But the faster you ask these rock stars to work, the more they will take shortcuts with each other. You hear them saying, "I just don't have the time to talk about that." That's the sound of the gap creaking open a little more.

But not talking makes things worse, and eventually the team spends more time managing the dysfunction arising from their me-you gaps than they do working on the project. And then you, boss, invest money, time and effort on process, or methods, or facilitators, or structure, to fix the mess. When you do that, it adds even more complexity and administration, but never really solves the underlying root cause.

That team of five of your very best people is going to end up exactly where many of your other project teams do: late, over budget, over schedule, mired in process and project meetings, miserable and cynical. And when they do finally deliver, it will probably be a compromise solution that satisfies no one.

That was a team of five. Now imagine the me-you gaps that exist in a team of ten or fifteen. Think of the gaps in an organization of several hundred or thousand! Have you noticed that large organizations can feel dehumanized, mechanistic, disengaged and process-bound? That's the gap multiplied hundreds and thousands of times.

And because human systems, like teams, departments, organizations and countries are fractal, self-similar at every level of abstraction, the me-you gap becomes the us-them gap. Management vs. employees, parents vs. kids, older vs. younger, central vs. regional, and all the other separations we organize around, are the offspring of the gap between you and me multiplied over and over.

Companies sometimes try to mechanize closing the gap using organizational processes and frameworks. But they are aiming too high.

Closing the me-you gap is individual, manual labor. It takes deliberate and focused work, by each of us, over every interaction we have, every day. The conversations that really matter, the ones that bring us close to one another, are intimate and contextual. They aren't the kinds of conversations we have in a training room.

Those intimate conversations typically happen after the team-building workshop is long over, in the moments of quiet and reflection, when we have time to ourselves, and freedom to choose with whom to connect. When we have freedom and safety in hallways, elevators, lunchrooms, on trains, and at the dinner table, we might open up a little.

But how often does the right atmosphere and right mood to have those private conversations appear? Increasingly we use every moment for "work," or achievement, or reaching for our goals. We have been trained to be "productive" rather than intentional.

Even when we have those moments when there's nothing to "do", we may want to hold them for ourselves, just for resting or recovering. We want to connect, *and* we want silence. We want intimacy, *and* we want safety. We want cooperation, *and* we want freedom.

Catching the right moment might take longer than we have. We need a reliable, repeatable way to skillfully use the time we have, as we work and live together, to intentionally close those gaps.

One me-you gap at a time, a team grows its trust, its agility and its collective genius. One me-you gap at a time, we connect intentionally with each other in a way that honors us as individuals and preserves our safety and freedoms.

The Core Commitments and Protocols (The Core) are basic rules and tools that support the deliberate and contextual two-person connections we need to make to be agile, creative, innovative and engaged.

This book is the guide to using the Core for the most challenging, rewarding work we will ever do together on a team: closing the me-you gap.

THE CORE TOOLS FOR CLOSING THE GAP

The newest computer can merely compound, at speed, the oldest problem in the relations between human beings, and in the end the communicator will be confronted with the old problem, of what to say and how to say it.
- Edward R. Murrow

We're going to close the me-you gap. We have to cover a long distance, and we'll go step by step. For the journey we need some rules of the road, some high quality tools, and some safety gear. We're going to do work that lets us practice using the tools. And then we're going to keep practicing so we master the tools and can feel comfortable using them in any situation.

The me-you gap is what keeps us from trusting one another before we have evidence of trustworthiness. It separates every person in the world from every other person in the world. We use it to protect ourselves, but it has the unintended consequence of isolating and holding us back from possibility.

I can't see inside you and you can't see inside me. Who we are inside is a mystery to others. Your hidden self is both potentially miraculous and dangerous to me if I need you to help me get something done, if I want you to be my friend, or if we are making a life together.

When I think of me, I think of what is available to me: memories, thoughts, feelings, swirling, ever changing, complex, multi-dimensional. I think of wants and resentments and dreams and images and contradictions and fears and visions.

When I think of you I also think of what is available to me, but it's a very different list. What's available to me about you is only what I can observe: what I have seen or heard in the past from you and about you, what I see or hear today, and how what is observable today contradicts or reinforces what I have seen or heard in the past.

I use whatever evidence I can find to help me know you better while maintaining my safety in your presence. And since I am an embodied bundle of emotional and physical experiences, psychological biases and contradictions, I make a lot of mistakes reading you. I imagine what you will do in the future, why you make the choices you do, and how that might affect me. But I will never, ever know what you know about you. You are hidden from me and will remain that way forever.

With this chasm of unknowns between us that we're constantly trying to navigate, it's no wonder interesting, and often unintended, things happen when we try to accomplish something together.

I might hide my ideas from you because I'm afraid no one cares as much about turning them into great products as I do. You might hide your feelings from me because you worry I'll think you're weak or needy. We could hide our wants from each other because we don't believe we'll ever achieve them and we're ashamed of our potential to fail. We sometimes assume things about each other that aren't true but could be. We dance around each other, taking a risk here, pulling back there, being curious one day, feeling offended the next, and wishing it were easier to trust each other and just get on with life.

All of this hiding, dancing, assuming, and reacting we do with each other multiplies over and over with every me-you relationship we have.

We are under tremendous pressure to work well together. The phrase "reach out to each other" is a common one in North American offices. Many of us have a legion of organizational development consultants and teamwork facilitators roaming our corridors, bookshelves groaning with books about how important trust is, and gurus charging thousands of dollars for more training and certifications in programs that are supposed to teach us how to solve these issues.

Yet most of the tools we use are incomplete or unsatisfying. And in many twenty-first century organizations we are still using antiquated, rusty, leftovers from the age of the factory when little or no interaction was required of us at all. As a result, in spite of the time we put into these programs and methods, our workplaces are vast, echoing Grand Canyons of me-you gaps.

Because we don't have helpful tools, we hope that simply being together is enough. We wait for our teams to "evolve" and hope that hiring the right people will help. We hire facilitators to march us through the ugly swampland of distrust to a promised land on the other side, but are often disappointed to discover the other side looks a lot like the place we came from. We turn managers into mom and dad to whom we complain when we're mean to each other, and then we complain about the managers when they can't make the pain go away.

The problem with delegating our trust building leadership to facilitators and managers is that anyone can cajole, plead, threaten and "motivate" me to communicate and share. But if I don't know *how* to trust, if I don't have trust skills that I know will help me, and if I'm scared of getting hurt when the manager or facilitator isn't around, then I'll keep doing what keeps me safe.

Those of us who experience this struggle between wanting to connect and wanting to stay free and safe know instinctively that there must be a way to get both. We may have had glimpses of collaboration that flowed, and work that felt respectful and supportive without losing its fun and openhearted ease.

There's something familiar each time that magic happens, as if the same elements were present creating a pattern of behaviour. But like the woodsman who couldn't see the forest for the trees, when we try to see those elements and what created them, they seem to be just outside our field of vision, out of focus and undefined. So we fall back on the assumption that great connections must come from blind good luck.

It takes an independent eye to see the forest, watching how people create patterns of freedom, trust, respect and support. That independent observation can reveal the familiar repeatable tools and rules that we can put in our toolbox to create connections with integrity, freedom, heart and purpose.

Jim and Michele McCarthy created the conditions to make those observations in 1996 when they began gathering data about patterns of skilful interpersonal behaviour that have come to be known as the Core Commitments and Protocols (the Core).

In an iterative laboratory experiment they observed what worked between people and what didn't when the participants tried to accomplish a project together. Using the same project over and over with team after team, they wrote down what they observed worked for everyone, regardless of culture, language, race, age, or nationality, and gave those observations to the next new team.

They then observed again, and continued to test, refine, test, refine with hundreds of teams and thousands of people worldwide in an experiment that continues today. The result has been used over and over, in working teams all over the world.

For many years, I have had the great honor to be one of the instructors who lead the laboratory experiment the McCarthys call BootCamp (from "booting" the new software, the Core Commitments and Protocols, in your head).

With my wonderful partner, Paul, we've watched teams in many countries, cultures and organizations learn and use the tools to be great on purpose. That environment is ideal for observing fundamental human behaviour. What we see in those teams was that the first problem every team member solved, even before closing the me-you gap, was the problem of "the I in team". But it wasn't the problem most people think it is.

They didn't pretend there *was* no I in team, ignore the "I", suppress it, or subordinate it to a theoretical higher purpose. What we saw was that the very core of the success of the team began with every person's focused attention on themselves: knowing and sharing what they wanted, thought, and felt.

For each team to truly excel, it needed each person to steward his or her own unique strengths, wisdom, ideas, passion, self-care, integrity, feelings, vision and connections. True shared purpose, the kind that powers the achievement of visions others believe are impossible, consistently emerged when the individuals used the Core Commitments and Protocols to intentionally and deliberately know and look after themselves. They then intentionally shared themselves and sought to understand one another, pair by pair.

Each person knew and shared him- or herself, sought to learn about others, maintained integrity, fulfilled promises, and practiced being vulnerable. From that simple set of resilient initial conditions, a web of complex, rich and powerful interconnections and trust emerged at a team level.

In fact, we realized that the web of connection between *pairs of people*, woven together intentionally, *was the team*. Once the team emerged from developing the one-to-one connections, time, meaning and vision were theirs to play with.

An outside expert couldn't build these teams. It wasn't the result of the right people being put together, or the right facilitator leading the brainstorming session. No facilitator could have led the team into connection that deep and lasting.

When individuals chose to learn and use the simple rules and tools of the Core Commitments and Protocols, they organized their own safe, rational, engaged and honest one-to-one connections at the time and in the space that was the most effective for them. A complex web of self-organizing shared leadership, shared vision, creative intimacy and rational mutual support emerged without the need for external control.

What I learned was that when we see a great team, what we see is a powerful web of me-you combinations that are carefully and intentionally cultivated, conversation-by-conversation, action-by-action.

This book is about how you can use the Core as your Do-It-Yourself trust, safety, freedom and accountability toolkit. It supports your freedom to choose what you participate in, to whom you speak, when you share, when you leave, and how you look after yourself. And it supports the people around you doing the same.

With these tools in our hands, we don't have to wait for random moments of connection, but can instead use these tools to create those moments on purpose.

We can intentionally create the conditions for the two of us to be trusting and trustworthy, safely exchanging what we want, think and feel. We can amplify trustworthy behaviours and dampen untrustworthy behaviours, and keep each other accountable to our promises.

When we can believe promises will be met, we don't have to micromanage each other. When we have a shared commitment, and a way to call out missed promises with compassion and integrity, we can stop rehearsing the painful conversations about confusion, misunderstandings, and failed accountability. Instead, we can use our mental and emotional energy to work on the things that are fascinating, exciting and energizing to us. When we are freed from mundane accountability control, we can make meaning together.

There's also a bigger result here, bigger than you and me. The pebble we drop in the ocean by closing the me-you gap will ripple out into every interaction we have, and every interaction our friends and colleagues have.

"You and I" are the basic building block of "us and them." Every me-you gap we close becomes a starting point for another gap to close. Our team and their team, our department and the other department, our company and our customers, our country and their country.

Me-you is more than an aggregate of our combined selves when we are able to trust. When we support each other to get what each of us wants, we generate a shared purpose that is larger than each of us individually, and becomes the essence of our team, our unique advantage.

If each of us then turned to the next couple of people, closed that gap, and they did the same, the world would feel richer, more meaningful, more familiar and safer in no time. So changing the world starts with the first two people. As I like to say, somebody has to go first.

Let it be us.

RULES OF THE ROAD: THE CORE COMMITMENTS

First say to yourself what you would be; and then
do what you have to do.
- Epictetus

We're on a journey, and when we're travelling it's helpful to adopt some simple universal principles for interacting with our fellow travelers regardless of our country or language.

The Core Commitments, a set of simple "rules of the road," are the basic principles of great teams, pairs and individuals as designed by people intending to close the me-you gap. The Core Protocols, the simple tools for the journey, are supported by and support the Commitments. I'll draw connections between the Commitments and Protocols throughout the book.

In this section, I'll talk a little about each Commitment one by one, and why it helps us close the me-you gap. To start us off, here is the full set of Core Commitments (Core Protocols version 3.03, www.liveingreatness.com)

The Core Commitments

1. I commit to engage when present.
   a. To know and disclose
      - what I want,
      - what I think, and
      - what I feel.
   b. To always seek effective help.
   c. To decline to offer and refuse to accept incoherent emotional transmissions.
   d. When I have or hear a better idea than the currently prevailing idea, I will immediately either

- propose it for decisive acceptance or rejection, and/or
- explicitly seek its improvement.

    e. I will personally support the best idea
    - regardless of its source,
    - however much I hope an even better idea may later arise, and
    - when I have no superior alternative idea.

2. I will seek to perceive more than I seek to be perceived.
3. I will use teams, especially when undertaking difficult tasks.
4. I will speak always and only when I believe it will improve the general results/effort ratio.
5. I will offer and accept only rational, results-oriented behavior and communication.
6. I will disengage from less productive situations
    - When I cannot keep these commitments,
    - When it is more important that I engage elsewhere.
7. I will do now what must be done eventually and can effectively be done now.
8. I will seek to move forward toward a particular goal, by biasing my behavior toward action.
9. I will use the Core Protocols (or better) when applicable.
    - I will offer and accept timely and proper use of the Protocol Check protocol without prejudice.
10. I will neither harm--nor tolerate the harming of--anyone for his or her fidelity to these commitments.
11. I will never do anything dumb on purpose.

1. ENGAGE WHEN PRESENT

I commit to engage when present.
    a. To know and disclose
- *what I want,*
- *what I think, and*
- *what I feel.*

    b. To always seek effective help.
    c. To decline to offer and refuse to accept incoherent emotional transmissions.
    d. When I have or hear a better idea than the currently prevailing idea, I will immediately either
- *propose it for decisive acceptance or rejection, and/or*
- *explicitly seek its improvement.*

    e. I will personally support the best idea
- *regardless of its source,*
- *however much I hope an even better idea may later arise, and*
- *when I have no superior alternative idea.*

What does engaging mean? Talking? Listening? Participating and helping? Yes, all of those. And it also means being present, both physically and mentally. It means putting down the phone, laptop, turning off the TV, taking off the headphones and really attending to the conversation or idea or action. It means not letting ourselves be distracted or mentally disengaging from what is going on in our presence.

It means knowing and gracefully sharing what's going on in our own heads, hearts, and guts so we take decisions that are aligned with our real selves and so that others can know our truths. It means asking for help when we've had our buttons pushed or when something has triggered an emotional reaction so we and others can keep our behaviour and emotions coherent, and know if a problem must be fixed, or comfort given, or new information sought, or joy celebrated. Knowing and sharing our best ideas, or actively supporting the ideas of others.

That takes skill, and the safety and freedom to rationally choose to engage when we can, Ask For Help when we need it, or disengage when we've run out of gas, or don't have the emotional or mental reserves to work toward positive results. The simple rules and tools of the Core Commitments and Protocols help us build skills and navigate the basics of engaging when present.

Let's go a little deeper with the first Commitment.

Know and disclose what you want, think and feel

Knowing and disclosing what you want, think and feel are at the heart of closing the me-you gap, the nucleus of the fundamental particle, and the reason the "I" in team is so critically important. Knowing and disclosing these three things will make you accessible, real and understandable to others. It will also make it much less tiring getting through each day.

It sucks a lot of energy out of us to be what we're not. If you're like many of us, you've been keeping what you want, think and feel pretty well hidden for years. You've created a kind of artificial intelligence version of yourself that your real self hides behind.

Unfortunately, the "real" self just keeps popping out, often at the most inappropriate times. When the "public" self and the "real" self switch, it can be embarrassing and confusing. The people around us wonder what else we're hiding, and what they'll have to deal with next. Being consistent, on the other hand, being integrated in our thinking and behaviour, is the beginning of being trustworthy. The only way to be consistent is to know who you are, and to reveal that to others.

If you know and disclose, which really means "reveal" or "share," what you want, think and feel all of a sudden, the people around you may be unnerved. They are expecting you to be that public persona, that cardboard cutout version of yourself.

Showing them what's really going on behind your eyeballs might be a really good thing from their perspective if you've been switching between the real you and the public you. But if your public persona has been rock solid, it might freak them out. They might even not like the real you.

Another possibility is that the people around you will be relieved that you finally make sense to them. You might find that they are more at ease, and are happy that they no longer have to guess what you're going to do next.

The skills of knowing and disclosing each of what we want, think and feel, take practice, especially if our default mode is to hide our real selves. We'll talk about tools to help us know and disclose what we want in the chapter on Personal Alignment, know and disclose what we think in the chapter on Investigate, and know and disclose what we feel in the chapter on Check In.

Always seek effective help

Asking for help is a magic tool for closing the me-you gap.

Asking someone for help nets you lots of benefits in one step. The easiest one to recognize is that if the person gives you the information you needed, you might get you work done faster this time, or from now on. But that's not all.

If you ask me for my ideas, insights, assistance, knowledge, capabilities, or skills, you show me that you think I'm worth connecting with, that you aren't trying to do everything yourself, and that you're open to receiving my help, even if it's only a quick conversation. Most importantly, it shows you're willing to be vulnerable, a clear step across the me-you gap.

When was the last time you asked someone at work if they had an idea that would help you get your job done faster? Or asked your husband to help with the laundry? Or asked your wife for help with roofing the house? Or asked your kids to help plan the family vacation?

Just this morning, Paul asked me to help him load some large logs in a truck to bring back to our house for our firewood. He likes cutting our firewood and has cut and loaded and unloaded and split and stacked a lot of wood over the years. Today, he could have done the work by himself. But these were big logs, and doing it alone would have taken more than twice the time it would take two people, hurt his back and left him cranky for the rest of the day.

Instead, because he asked me for help and I said yes, it took us twenty minutes, was easy and companionable for us both, and the neighbor whose truck we had borrowed was delighted to see it returned so fast.

Would you ask me for help in this situation? You might.

On the other hand, you might not want to interrupt me, or have me hurt myself. Or you might want to impress me, and yourself, by doing it all alone. Or you might think I won't do it "right". Or you might not be willing to wait while I finish my own work and get ready.

Now substitute any job for loading wood in a truck: finishing a project task; getting a pile of work done that's in your inbox; doing the laundry; roofing the house.

When we don't Ask For Help, it can be because we want to keep the rewards to ourselves. The rewards can be monetary, but they can also be identity, pleasure, power and more. Being able to complain about how difficult it was to do it all alone is a reward for some people.

Many of us identify ourselves with solo accomplishment. That just makes sense. We spend the first 18 to 25 years of our lives being graded, and then we go to work and get paid individually for what we do. We want to prove ourselves worthy of salaries, promotions, awards, admiration, respect, obligation, and pats on the back. At home, we want love, power, and respect.

What will you think if I ask for help? That I'm lazy, incompetent, or stupid? I'm trying to get you to do my work for me? I need to go figure it out myself, just like you did? I need to pay my dues? I need to learn to be more self-reliant? I need to stop being needy?

Is that what you would really think of me if I asked you for help, or is that what you're afraid other people will think of you if you ask for help?

Let's go back to Paul, the firewood, and me. We got it done fast, had fun, didn't get injured, did it in less than half the time it would have taken one person and we got the truck back to its owner so he could use it sooner.

Translate those benefits back to work. If I ask you for help, each of us might spend less time. Perhaps you spend a little more time now, but you'll probably spend less time later, because I'll know what to do and you won't have to get involved again. And we might come to a brilliant shared idea that saves us both, or even the entire company, time. There might be less risk of injury, misunderstanding, overwork, or unnecessary work. We can deliver our results faster so others aren't waiting for us. And we enjoy a shared experience that closes the gap and prepares us for even more fluid and skilful connections in future.

And there's the key. When we explicitly Ask For Help, we reveal our vulnerability, we get to see others in action, we share learning and creating, and we give each other a chance to be supportive, and to be supported. Each of those things, on its own, would bring us a little closer. But we get all of them at once when we just ask.

We'll talk more about this tool and how it works to support the Commitment "always seek effective help", in the Protocol Ask For Help.

Decline to offer and refuse to accept incoherent emotional transmissions.

Incoherent emotional transmissions sound like this:
"Where were you?"
"You sound upset."
"I'm not upset. I just want to know where you were."
"I was having lunch with a friend."
"What friend?"
"Does it matter?"

'Yes, of course it does. What do you mean, 'does it matter?' You're always out doing something with someone else and I have to keep this place running all by myself."

"So you are upset."

"No I'm not upset, dammit! Stop saying that!"

In the same situation, someone who didn't *offer* incoherent emotional transmissions might sound like this:

"I'm angry and afraid because I unexpectedly had to manage the client meeting alone and a some guy called while you were out to say he wants to talk to you about a job in Dubai. Will you tell me where you were at lunch?"

Someone who didn't *accept* incoherent emotional transmissions might say,

"It seems like this isn't a good time to talk about this. I'm going to Check Out. I'll be back in about an hour, if you want to continue the discussion then.""

Coherence, and behaving rationally, help close the me-you gap. If we can coherently share what we want, feel, and think, we create an environment of respect, reliability and accountability. And if we can't be coherent, we can leave gracefully, allowing everyone else to continue being safe and productive.

The Protocols Check In and Check Out help us keep the Commitment "to decline to offer and refuse to accept incoherent emotional transmissions."

Propose, improve and support the best idea

When I have or hear a better idea than the currently prevailing idea, I will immediately either

- *propose it for decisive acceptance or rejection, and/or*
- *explicitly seek its improvement.*

I will personally support the best idea
- *regardless of its source,*
- *however much I hope an even better idea may later arise, and*
- *when I have no superior alternative idea.*

The inside of your head is an infinite space. You can think up anything about anything. But how do you get those ideas out there so they can be heard and evaluated seriously, and make them as awesome as they can be once they're out? Closing the me-you gap and creating a clean exchange about ideas between you and others makes both more likely.

First you have to let go of the idea that only some people, the people who had special fairy dust sprinkled over their heads at birth, have the best ideas.

You know how the thinking goes: They went to the right schools, have the talent, the right tools, got attention from the right people, got the lucky break, have the right connections.

It's all nonsense.

Anyone can have a great idea. You might only have one incredibly, awesomely, magnificently, great idea in your life. That's all you need. And what we need, the rest of us, is for you to get that idea out so we can use it.

Have it, tell it to the world, and then support it. Defend it from all the people who say you don't have the right qualifications to have great ideas, or you use the wrong methodology to have great ideas, or you hang out with the wrong people to have great ideas.

Here are the flashing neon lights: A great idea is a great idea. It doesn't matter what school you went to, who you know, what people you hang around with - none of that matters. Repeat this to yourself. No one will care about any of that if you get that idea to work. So, get it to work fast. Make a decision, get support, and take action.

The tools Decider, for getting the idea heard and supported, and Perfection Game, a way to improve ideas, both support this Commitment to propose, improve and support the best idea.

2: SEEK TO PERCEIVE
MORE THAN YOU SEEK TO BE PERCEIVED

The second commitment is to seek to perceive more than you seek to be perceived.

Seeking to be perceived more than perceive, the opposite of this Commitment, sounds like this:

"How was your vacation?"

"It was great. We went to -"

"You went to Mexico, right? We went there too! We loved it! But I think this year we're going to somewhere different, because, you know, the food really wasn't that great, didn't you think, and the room was a bit small even though we had the presidential suite. So this year we're going to kayak to Antarctica to breed penguins blah, blah, blah."

Instead, meeting the commitment might look like this:

"How was your vacation?"

"It was great. We went to this cool little jazz club on the Tuesday and saw some great local musicians."

"Wow! What was cool about it for you?"

At work, not perceiving sounds like:

"I'm having problems with Joe. He's been missing project meetings."

"Oh, I know what you're going through. I've moved past all of that. When I was your age I used to worry about every problem that cropped up on the team. I used to lie awake at night, worrying and planning and fretting. These days I worry about things that are more important than that, things like blah, blah, blah."

Meeting the commitment at work might look like this:

"I'm having problems with Joe. He's been missing project meetings."

"It sounds like you don't like his behaviour. Is that accurate?" Nods. "What could you do about that?"

"Well, I could ask him what it would take for him to come to the meetings, or maybe ask him if he has an idea about making the meetings worth his time. He's a really important person on this project, and probably has lots of ideas that would help us."

"What else could you do?"

Again, perceiving is about suspending our own need to be heard in order to hear others. This is one of the easiest ways to close the me-you gap because it gives me information, and it gives you the rare opportunity to talk to someone who is genuinely interested in you. We'll talk about how to fulfill the Commitment "I will seek to perceive more than I seek to be perceived" with the Protocol Investigate.

3: USE TEAMS,
ESPECIALLY WHEN UNDERTAKING DIFFICULT TASKS

Difficult is different for everyone.

Writing might be difficult for some. Managing teams, working with people, coming up with ideas, working with numbers, working with words, remembering details, seeing the big picture. Each of these is easy for someone and difficult for someone else.

One person may hate filling in forms because it doesn't feel creative; another may love it, because it feels organized and certain. One person may hate speaking in public because they feel embarrassed at being the centre of attention; another may love it because they have ideas they want to share with many people and that's the fastest way to do it.

Teams are webs of freedom and trust that allow minds to open safely. As the me-you gaps begin to close, one-to-one, and the team begins to create a web of connections, using teams gives you access to more skills and ideas than you could ever have alone.

Teams can be your siblings when you're going through a life transition. They can be neighbors if you need help with getting chores done. You and your partner are a team.

Teams give support, help you stay accountable to your own goals, give you a useful outlet for your crazy ideas, and are an endless source of fascination, joy and fun.

Find individuals and close the gap with them. Then find more people, and close the gap with them. Your team is that web of connections. We'll talk about how to fulfill the Commitment "use teams, especially when undertaking difficult tasks" in the chapter on the Protocol Ask For Help.

4: SPEAK ALWAYS AND ONLY WHEN YOU BELIEVE IT WILL IMPROVE THE GENERAL RESULTS/EFFORT RATIO

Unless your job is public speaking, most people don't want to hear you talk, they want you to listen. Finding someone who will stop talking long enough to genuinely listen to you is as rare as a miracle. When was the last time you felt truly listened to?

I had a friend who told me once that when she and I first started having really deep conversations I listened so closely to her, and made her feel so listened to, she thought it was a trick. No one had ever actually listened to her before without being dismissive, giving advice, trying to solve her problem, or trying to one-up her with their own story.

She told me that after spending enough time with me she finally realized what I was doing was consistent in every conversation we had – it wasn't a game for me. And it was consistent with the rest of the way I behaved, which made her feel more comfortable about it, and let her just enjoy it. She stopped being suspicious about how closely I listened to her, but now she was intrigued – how did I do it, what was I doing, and why was it so powerful?

She decided to go to BootCamp, where she had a chance to work on a team using the Core to achieve something together. She said she finally "got it." She said she had seen the incredible results one can get by being fully present when someone else is talking. She said it takes a lot of energy and focus, but she has begun using the tools herself with great results.

Have you ever had someone focus his entire presence on you and what you have to say? Someone who doesn't talk to fill the silence, or hurry you along by finishing your sentences? Someone who asks questions not because they have an agenda about you, but because you are genuinely interesting to them?

It happens when we fall in love. The other person becomes our greatest fascination. We don't need to be in love to listen like that, but it does help to be genuinely curious, to be fascinated by what is inside the other person.

Why don't we get this chance more often? I believe we've institutionalized being perceived. Meetings have become agreement factories, each person taking his or her five, ten or twenty minutes to reiterate again what has already been said in order to have his or her voice added to the pot. Playing the meeting game usually involves being the loudest, the last, the most frequent or the most passionate.

How many times do we walk out of meetings lonelier than when we walked in? How many times is the best idea lost in the sea of voices? How often do we leave a meeting feeling tired, defeated and hopeless?

And even outside work, "for your own good" and "just sayin'" are key phrases that signal someone claiming their time to be perceived. Unsolicited feedback has been institutionalized as an annual performance review between boss and employee and as an argument strategy between spouses or between parents and kids. The moment to change may be long past, but we give the feedback anyway. Yet, too often "feedback" is a chance to tell someone, for *our* own good, to stop doing something we don't like.

We are taught it's better to "help" someone we think is struggling, rather than seeking to perceive the person and their struggle. Then we complain when the "help" is undervalued because it wasn't noticed, ignored because it was irrelevant, or actively rejected because it interfered with work already underway.

Seeking to perceive more than to be perceived is a way to counter each of these blocks to closing the me-you gap. Instead of giving feedback or "helping" without being asked, we can put our energy into truly being curious about each other, listening to the work that's already being done, and supporting that work by asking open-ended questions that invite the other's own solutions, satisfy our own curiosity and close the me-you gap. Once the gap begins to close, real, self-directed growth may take place in a spirit of freedom and trust.

How we listen, and how much we listen, changes how we trust and are trusted. To listen to others often and deeply takes courage and integrity, two virtues that shine out without a word being said and which create an environment of ease. We are attracted to people with those virtues because we sense we will be safe with them.

The Investigate Protocol helps fulfill the Commitment to "seek to perceive more than be perceived."

5: OFFER AND ACCEPT ONLY RESULTS-ORIENTED BEHAVIOUR AND COMMUNICATION

All of the tools in our toolbox support this Commitment. In fact, this Protocol sums up the Core. It's a set of simple rules and tools that help us be rational and accountable in our thoughts, words, and actions. This book is specifically about behaving and communicating wisely one-to-one, using the Core to get there, and because of that, closing the me-you gap.

I'll know what I want, think, and feel and share those things with you in a way that's coherent and consistent. I'll be present and engaged when I can and leave when I can't. I'll ask for your help, and any other help that might help. I'll ask more than tell. I'll support your idea, or offer a better one. I'll look for ways to improve the ideas we have together. I'll say what has to be said if it helps, and I won't say what I know won't help. I'll keep moving toward the goals we have together. I'll use tools that work, and check our commitments with each other. And I won't do anything dumb on purpose.

Sounds pretty rational to me.

6: LEAVE IF NECESSARY

I will disengage from less productive situations

- *When I cannot keep these commitments,*

- *When it is more important that I engage elsewhere.*

Have you ever been in an argument that became an argument about the argument? Or realized in a meeting that someone just said your name and everyone is looking at you and you've been daydreaming for ten minutes? Or you are anxious to leave because your daughter's recital is about to start, and your colleague is droning on and on about the same issue he was talking forty minutes ago?

Or the alternative may also have happened to you, as it has to me. You are so passionate about the subject that you're about to burst, so you interrupt everything your partner says? Your partner's eyes begin to glaze over and you become offended by her indifference. You feel the heat rise in your face, and you get ready for a fight. There's no way you're going to leave until she hears you out.

If it seems like a good time to leave, it probably is. If it seems like you'll explode if you leave, that's probably a good time to leave as well.

Leaving has a bad rap. We don't like to leave because something interesting might happen when we're gone. Someone might assign work to us.

I worry you might think you've won if I leave before I've had the last word. Or I worry that you'll think I'm a quitter.

You can always say no to the work later. You can come back to the conversation ready to resolve instead of argue. And if winning is the only reason you want to stay, it's time to shut down the conversation anyway.

If leaving is really the best idea in the long run, do it.

The Protocols Pass and Check Out are the tools to support this Commitment to "disengage from less productive situations," and we'll talk about them in Safety Gear For Closing The Gap.

7: DO NOW WHAT MUST BE DONE EVENTUALLY AND CAN EFFECTIVELY BE DONE NOW

Commitment #7 tells us to turn ideas into action.

There is a time to talk and a time to do when we're closing the gap. We not only learn about each other by talking and listening, we learn about each other in action, when we have work to do, when we need each other's help, when we ask for ideas, make decisions, and take action. We see each other's competence, preferences, passions and integrity in the work of making something together, whether it's designing a financial software system or baking a cake.

When we spend all our time repeating the same old conversations, weighing risks, trying to get to consensus, certainty, and detailed plans, we lose the opportunity to see each other's genius in action.

Instead, mix up the talking with doing. Once you get into action, intentionally practice the skills that will increase coherence and trust, like Investigate, Check In, Ask For Help, Perfection Game, and the safety protocols, Pass, Check Out, Intention Check, and Protocol Check.

It's also just smart to get things done sooner rather than later. When we've used our time well, we have time to share our work with each other and Ask For Help within, and outside, our own team before deadlines make us crazy.

Once we get into action we can use many different protocols to support all the Commitments. The Decider Protocol is one tool that explicitly supports this Commitment to "do now what must be done eventually, and can effectively done now," and quickly moves us from ideas to action.

8: KEEP MOVING TOWARD THE GOAL

I will seek to move forward toward a particular goal, by biasing my behavior

toward action.

Once you're taking action, it's so easy to get stuck. We get stuck in the past, in indecision, in wanting to be right, or liked, or certain, in wanting to know the future, in frameworks, in wishful thinking. We get stuck when we don't look after ourselves, so we get tired and cranky and lose our resilience for adapting. We get stuck focusing on what isn't working, what's holding us back, what we could do if only we had more of *something*.

We get stuck believing that if it's never been done before, it never will be done and it's not worth trying, our culture won't accept it, we don't do things like that here, we didn't invent it so it couldn't possibly work for us, it works for those other people but we're different.

We get stuck thinking that if we can get more information and more data, or have a stronger process, or methodology, or software, we'll have less risk and it will be safer to move forward. We get stuck thinking that we need to control each other, be in the same room together all the time, get everyone's input, whether they care or not. We get stuck thinking someone else will fix what's wrong, that we just need to find the right consultant, facilitator, manager, or employee.

But getting unstuck is really simple, in the end. It starts with us. You and me. Then you and him, and me and her. And on and on. Taking action, asking for help, learning, trusting.

Try stuff. Then try something else. Those who want to participate will catch up and those who don't won't slow you down. Never wait for consensus – trying to get there will kill your momentum, your spirit and your connection. Instead, make a version. Then improve it. Drop what isn't working; if it's a really great idea, it will come back all on its own. Learn from the version and try again. Share your genius. Don't hold back. Action is the teacher.

The Protocols Decider and Ask For Help are some of the tools that help us fulfill this Commitment to "seek to move forward toward a particular goal, by biasing my behavior toward action." But in the end, the entire toolbox of the Core Protocols is available to us to close the gap, and that, ultimately is what this is all about.

9: USE THE CORE OR BETTER

I will use the Core Protocols (or better) when applicable.

- *I will offer and accept timely and proper use of the* Protocol

  Check *protocol without prejudice.*

The key word in Commitment #9 is *use. Use* the Core Protocols or better.

Use them up. Try every different combination of the Protocols. Try the same Protocol with different me-you gaps and see what's the same and what's different. *Use* the Commitments and Protocols until they are worn out, and you have nothing left to learn, no new situation to try them on, nothing about fulfilling the Commitments you can't achieve with ease, no virtue you haven't tried as a Personal Alignment, no Protocol you haven't tried everywhere you go. Master the Core. Then decide if there's something better to use.

Since 2003 Paul and I have been using the Core Commitments and Protocols every day, for home and for work. We use them with people who know them and use them every day and people who have never heard of them; people who we like and trust and people we don't. We use them with each other, implicitly when things are flowing easily, and explicitly when we're stuck.

When we're using them perfectly, we'll let you know, but don't hold your breath.

The Core Commitments and Protocols are subject to comparison with other approaches. One of the things we find with the Core is that people with a passing familiarity, or no familiarity at all with actually using the Core to accomplish something with others, judge what they know of the Core to be "like" something they already use, or have rejected.

Every single person I have ever spoken to has compared the Core to whatever approach with which they are most familiar. That is interesting to me, because it means the Core is universal and works with all other approaches. People who learn the Core more seriously usually continue by saying, "But the Core is cleaner, more simple, more fundamental, more comprehensive. It's a complete set of foundational behaviours that works."

Yet, what we see is that the people who pass early judgment without actually trying the tools are dismissive; the Core is deceptively simple. Others look only for a specific answer for their specific itch, and don't see all the other possibilities. They use one of the Protocols and stop there. Michele McCarthy has a great metaphor for this: "It's as if they're at a banquet and have only found the raisins."

Those who use it, on the other hand, the ones who really work with it, try it, apply it, who treat it as a system of rules and tools that work together like the rules and tools of chess or poker - those are the people who reap the rewards.

So, the most important word in this Commitment is "use". *Use* the Commitments and Protocols. Try them. Pretend they work. Try them in many situations, with many people; at home, at work, in the street, on the train, or in the school lunchroom.

Use them. In fact, use them until you are so familiar with them they feel like old boots, comfortable and polished. Then, if something better comes along, try it too.

10: DON'T HURT PEOPLE FOR KEEPING COMMITMENTS

I will neither harm--nor tolerate the harming of--anyone for his or her fidelity to

these commitments.

Harming someone can be subtle. It can come out as sabotaging their work, making every conversation difficult, scapegoating them, shunning, isolating, and laughing at them, goading them into Checking Out, shaming or embarrassing them.

Tolerating others being harmed can come out as apathy or staying silent when the harm occurs.

It takes presence, courage, self-awareness, integrity and all the other virtues to practice any commitment to anything, whether it's a relationship, a vocation or a set of principles, every day. Respect the folks who work at it. And don't tolerate disrespect to you or anyone else. In the end, no matter what it is, don't hurt anyone for committing to something, especially to simple rules that help close the me-you gap. Better yet, support them and try the tools yourself.

There are Safety Protocols that specifically support the safety of people wanting to try the Core Protocols and Commitments. The ones that specifically apply to this Commitment not to "harm - nor tolerate the harming of - anyone for his or her fidelity to these commitments," are Protocol Check and Intention Check. We'll look at them in the section called Safety Gear For The Journey.

11: NEVER DO ANYTHING DUMB ON PURPOSE

This is the hardest commitment. Also the greatest.

Doing something dumb *intentionally* looks like this:

Pretending to know how long something will take if you've never done it before just because I asked you to tell me.

Staying in my meeting when it's going nowhere because you think I'll be offended if you leave.

Not telling me how you feel because you don't want me to be upset.

Neglecting your health in order to work more hours so that I will be impressed with how busy you are.

Tolerating me not delivering on my promises because you don't want to confront me.

Keeping a fight going because it's more important for me to see you're right than for us to move on.

Blaming me for you not getting what you want.

Not checking out of an argument when you can't think rationally because you don't want me to think I've won.

Saying yes when you really want to say no because you want me to like you.

Not asking for my help because you want me to see you as a hero, smart enough to figure it out alone.

Lying because you're afraid of what I will think of you if I knew the truth.

Being resentful and jealous of me, because I am getting what I want.

I've done all of these things. Probably most of us have. And we all know that the consequences can be terrible. So we're not going to do them. Or any other dumb thing we might be tempted to do on purpose.

SAFETY GEAR FOR CLOSING THE GAP

It is not change that causes anxiety; it is the feeling that we are without defenses in the presence of what we see as danger that causes anxiety.
- Robert Kegan and Lisa Laskow Lahey

Now that we've got a simple set of rules, The Core Commitments, we're going to start learning the Core Protocols, the tools that support us keeping these Commitments. The first tools we'll learn are going to be our safety gear, the Protocols we use to look after ourselves and to be successful.

For each of the Protocols, I'll give some ideas about using the Protocol to close the me-you gap, and then give you the full text of that protocol.

Let's jump into the first Protocol, Pass, in the next section, Safety Gear For Closing The Gap

PASS

Life is the sum of all your choices.
- Albert Camus

Pass is the first Safety Protocol we'll look at, and as with each Protocol, I'll include the full text of the Protocol below the section.

Pass is useful when you're not sure you want to participate in an activity or a conversation, or if you're sure you don't want to participate. Pass gives you the chance to gracefully decline an invitation without having to explain why.

Here's an example of how you could use Pass:

Annie and Pat just met at work. Pat's worked and lived all around the world, has a loyal following of friends and colleagues and commands any room she enters. Annie's quieter, more contained. Annie really likes Pat's outgoing personality; she's funny, brave and doesn't let people push her around. Annie wants to figure out what makes Pat tick. But Annie is afraid that Pat will steamroller her. She knows Pat likes to do crazy things like skydiving and whitewater rafting. What if Pat asks her along? If she says no, will Pat tease her for being too timid? She's seen Pat do that before.

Annie knows the Pass protocol. If Pat invites her along she can just say, "I Pass," without justifying herself or explaining anything. Then she realizes that knowing and sharing what she wants, thinks and feels, being sure of herself, saying out loud that she's Passing on what she doesn't want to do, is just the kind of strength she admires in Pat.

She also realizes she can use Pass with colleagues at work. The next time someone asks for volunteers for a committee (which Annie hates) she can Pass.

People who are used to bullying and manipulating are often unnerved when you use the Pass Protocol. Don't be surprised if you encounter some resistance, teasing, or coercion when you Pass. Just remember, you have the freedom to choose what you spend your time doing. Keep saying, "I Pass" if that's what you want. And if you have to, use the next safety protocol, Check Out to leave the conversation physically.

Now that you have a tool in your safety gear, you can take responsibility for your own safety crossing the gap. That should feel really good.

The Simple Tool: Pass Protocol

The Pass protocol is how you decline to participate in something. Use it anytime you don't want to participate in an activity.

Steps
1. When you've decided not to participate, say "I Pass."
2. Unpass any time you desire. Unpass as soon as you know you want to participate again by saying "I unpass."

Commitments
- Hold reasons for Passing private.
- Pass on something as soon as you are aware you are going to Pass.
- Respect the right of others to Pass without explanation.
- Support those who Pass by not discussing them or their Pass.
- Do not judge, shame, hassle, interrogate or punish anyone who Passes.

Notes
- In general, you will not be in good standing with your Core Commitments if you Pass most of the time.
- You can Pass on any activity; however, if you have adopted the Core Commitments, you cannot Pass on a Decider vote and you must say "I'm in" when checking in.
- You can Pass even though you have already started something

CHECK OUT

To argue with a man who has renounced the use and authority of reason is like administering medicine to the dead.
- Thomas Paine

Let's look at some more opportunities to use the safety gear. Are any of these familiar?

You're in the middle of one of those low-blood-sugar arguments with your partner and just about to say something you'd regret later?

You're in a meeting and everyone's stopped really listening to each other, and the usual suspects are talking on and on, mutually agreeing without actually making a decision, while the interns warm the chairs and surreptitiously check their text messages?

You're at a family gathering and Uncle Harold is on bottle number two, your cousin's new boyfriend has been telling you corporate war stories for the past hour, the nephews are beating up the neighbor kid, and the women have all retreated to the kitchen to complain about their husbands?

You've been here. I know you have. Or at least, if not here, then at least you've been in a neighboring country. And every time you go back you feel you need full combat gear.

This is a great time to use safety tool number two: Check Out.

Check Out was designed for leaving gracefully. You can use it when you shouldn't be here, or you should be somewhere else. It supports the Commitment to behave and communicate rationally, and helps close the gap because when you don't tolerate or participate in what drives you crazy, others will begin to see you as having reliable integrity.

I use the tool Check Out when I know that if I stay I'll say or do something that I'll regret. I also Check Out if I think someone else will say or do something I'll regret. When my "lizard brain" tells me this isn't a person in front of me, it's a saber-toothed tiger, I know it's time to vamoose. If I stay, I'm going to do a lot of damage to others and probably, in the long term, to myself. That's just going to widen the gap, not narrow it.

The saber-toothed tiger isn't likely to ask where you're going or worry about why you're upset, but Uncle Harold or your colleague from the Marketing Department might. This is where Check Out is golden.

Check Out explicitly says, don't explain, apologize or justify your actions. The reason? If you're ready to Check Out, it's time to turn off the mouth. Don't stick around to talk about it, just Check Out. Chances are no one will care if you leave anyway. Few will even notice if you do it right.

Well, your partner might notice. He or she might be enjoying the drama of the argument, looking forward to the next volley of blame, and will be confused and frustrated that you're leaving. She might accuse you of running away. He might accuse you of avoiding the subject. But if you know you just can't stop yourself from saying something you'll both regret later, just Check Out.

When you learn to Check Out it's almost a given that the people around you will learn from you and try Check Out themselves. So, Check Out with the same grace and kindness you hope they will show you when you're the one left behind. Say, "I'm checking out," simply, gracefully and without blame, a raised voice, or emotional drama. Don't get pulled back in. Just keep walking and close the door gently on your way out.

While you're checked out, get what you need to come back ready for human contact again. Take a walk, go for a run, or read a book. I like to work out hard with really heavy weights so that I'm completely exhausted when I come back. Usually, by then, all the adrenaline is out of my system and I don't have the energy to fight. I've usually also figured out what it was that got me so angry in the first place, and I can talk rationally about solving the problem, instead of feeding the drama.

If you left because there were more important things you could be doing, then maybe you don't need to come back quickly. You can choose how to use your time, knowing that the folks you leave will do their best to make a good decision and take action. When you come back, close the gap to find out what that decision was, and support or improve it.

I know of some folks who don't like Check Out. They say it seems "dangerous" to them, and might hurt consensus. When I hear that, the red warning light goes off.

What could possibly be dangerous about me taking my unskillful, reactive self somewhere else, so that you don't have to be in my presence while I'm incoherent? Or taking my distracted, pre-occupied self away from the action so you can get on with more important things than managing my bad mood? If you trust me, you know I'll come back refreshed and ready to be fully engaged. If you want to keep me there, or I believe I'm indispensible and the world will end if I leave, something's wrong with our trust. We need to stop, and close the gap again.

Decisions and action will continue while I'm gone, and I know that. If I come back from being checked out I know I need to catch up and help. And I trust you to make great decisions while I'm gone. We have tools to get to that kind of trust, so read on.

Simple Tool: Check Out Protocol

Check Out requires that your physical presence always signifies your engagement. You must Check Out when you are aware that you cannot maintain the Core Commitments or whenever it would be better for you to be elsewhere.

Steps

1. Say, "I'm checking out."
2. Physically leave the group until you're ready to Check In once again.
3. Optionally, if it is known and relevant, you can say when you believe you'll return.
4. Those who are present for the Check Out may not follow the person, talk to or about the person checking out or otherwise chase him or her.

Commitments

- Return as soon as you can and are able to keep the Core Commitments.
- Return and Check In without unduly calling attention to your return.
- Do not judge, shame, hassle, interrogate, or punish anyone who checks out.

Notes

- When you Check Out do it as calmly and gracefully as possible so as to cause minimal disruption to others.
- Check Out if your emotional state is hindering your success, if your receptivity to new information is too low, or if you do not know what you want.
- Check Out is an admission that you are unable to contribute at the present time.

INTENTION CHECK

People aren't either wicked or noble. They're like chef's salads, with good things and bad things chopped and mixed together in a vinaigrette of confusion and conflict.
- Lemony Snicket, The Grim Grotto

Our motivations are complex. Sometimes not even *we* are sure why we do what we do. And it's hard for others to know our intent at the best of times. So sometimes, when someone's behaviour is just odd or unexpected, we just need a way to ask, gracefully and without assumption, "What is your intent?"

Here's an example:

Nina and Larry are getting a presentation ready for the boss. Larry's new to the organization and still trying to make his mark. Nina decides to put the bones of the presentation together herself and then show it to Larry to get his feedback. Larry is upset that Nina has stolen his chance to show what he can do, and taken away his first chance to shine in front of the boss.

Nina says, "I just wanted to make it easier for you since you're new here and you don't know what the boss will be looking for."

This is true, *and* what Nina didn't say was that she did the work herself so she didn't have to listen to and incorporate Larry's new ideas. She assumed it would take longer to work with him than it would take to just do it herself. Nina, like the rest of us is a complex person. Larry could just make some assumptions, but his opportunity is to ask her what her intent was, and begin to close the gap with an honest conversation that feeds their future working relationship.

If someone is behaving in a way that seems strange to you, instead of assuming, ask what their intent was. Assumptions are often wrong because, as we said at the beginning, I can't see inside you, or you inside me, no matter how close we are. We need to use words to share our complex selves. Plus, asking is another chance to close the me-you gap.

Here are some examples. You're having lunch with your mother. She says, "There's this nice girl I want you to meet." You think her intent is to get you married so you'll have grandkids. Her real intent is to find you someone to go out with so you're not so lonely. Your unspoken assumption about her intent will drive a very different conversation with her than the one you'll have if you just ask her what her intent is. If you ask, you'll have the chance to have a much more interesting, real and positive conversation than the one you're likely to have in your head for the next few days if you simply stay on your side of the gap.

You're talking to a sales guy about the product you're working on and he says, "I heard you're working on our next killer product. You must be pretty proud of it." Is he asking because he's impressed, or because he wants to sell it to customers before it's even finished, putting unnecessary pressure on you and your team? Just ask. Maybe he can help you. Maybe he has ideas about what the customers want that could help the team. Maybe he's just genuinely happy for you. But you'll never know until you take that step.

And sometimes, the other person's intent really is worrisome. That's good to know too. By asking you open the door to information that helps you know if this is a person with whom you want to continue to close the gap. You might see resistance to telling the truth, lying, blaming and deflection. All of those things are information that will support your safety and freedom. And you just have to ask.

Instead of spending days, nights and weekends anticipating the unknown, just ask. Asking doesn't hurt, it might clear the air, and you'll be closing the gap.

Simple Tool: Intention Check Protocol

Use Intention Check to clarify the purpose of your own or another's behavior. Use it when you aren't expecting a positive outcome resulting from the current behavior. Intention Check assesses the integrity of your own and another's intention in a given case.

Steps

1. Ask, "What is your/my intention with X?" where X equals some type of actual or pending behavior to the person whose intention you want to know.
2. If it would be helpful, ask "What response or behavior did you want from whom as X?"

Commitments

- Be aware of your own intention before checking the intention of another.
- Investigate sufficiently to uncover the intention of the person or his actions.
- Make sure you have the intention to resolve any possible conflict peacefully before intention checking someone else. If you do not have a peaceful intention, Check Out.
- Do not be defensive when someone asks you what your intention is. If you can't do this, Check Out.

Notes

If conflict arises that seems irresolvable, Check Out and Ask For Help.

PROTOCOL CHECK

Beyond right and wrong, there is a field. I will meet you there.
- Rumi

We're not perfect. We goof, forget, slip up, make mistakes, and take shortcuts.

When time is tight, or we're tired or hungry, it's easy to break commitments. The gap opens up not because we've made the mistake, but because no one calls it out into the open and makes it part of the ongoing conversation.

Tolerating broken promises guarantees promises will be broken again, and that's poison for closing the gap. Instead we need to clearly note broken promises, understand how to get back on track and decide what will change so it doesn't happen again.

But first we each need to agree on a common set of rules, like the rules of the road or the rules in chess or baseball. We've already talked about the Core Commitments in the chapter "Rules of the Road" The Core Commitments are the rules that seem to work well over all cultures, languages, and other differences as the common foundation for closing the me-you gap. So in the spirit of doing what works even though it wasn't "invented here," we've agreed to adopt the Core Commitments.

In fact, they're the rules of the game as described by most of the major philosophers, thinkers and leaders throughout history. There's really no surprise there. The Core Commitments and Protocols are the product of hundreds of groups of people trying to deliver great products and services together, on time, every time, with little time; they are a complete system of universally effective behaviours that feels as familiar as it is revolutionary.

What happens when we all voluntarily agree to use those rules, and then do something different in practice? When you play cards or chess or Go or baseball, you agree at the beginning – rationally - to use the rules of the game. The rules give you a way to avoid negotiating every single move. It speeds up play, and lets you enjoy the interaction, without worrying about structure all the time.

When you're playing chess and your partner moves her knight the way a bishop should move, or when you're playing baseball and the guy on second base runs straight to home, what do you do? Usually, you say, "The rule is..." and you're both on track again. But when we work together or enjoy a relationship we're often confused about what rules we should expect each other to follow, and what to say when we think an agreed rule is broken.

For instance, if I usually call you at 10 am, and today I don't, what can you do? Was there an agreement? Did I break a promise? If there was an agreement, will you remind me of it and ask what happened, or just ignore it and hope it doesn't happen again?

Often, instead of dealing directly with the person on the other side of the me-you gap, we avoid "conflict" about the ambiguous agreement and instead take our frustrations to friends, colleagues, managers, parents and partners. All we're doing by avoiding checking the agreement is causing drama, wasting time, and leaving the real problem untouched.

If we don't have clear commitments, a way to remind each other of what we've committed to gracefully, and a way to reset expectations when we break those commitments, we risk the gap opening up simply through neglect.

Rather than descending into the common practice of complaining, judging character, and claiming who's right and wrong, we're going to use Protocol Check. This Protocol is a graceful and compassionate reminder of our commitments to each other and of our commitment to use the protocols. It's also a calm, non-threatening way for us to confirm our mutual understanding of the Core Commitments and Protocols.

Simple Tool: Protocol Check Protocol

Use Protocol Check when you believe a protocol is being used incorrectly in any way or when a Core Commitment is being broken.

Steps

1. Say "Protocol Check."
2. If you know the correct use of the protocol, state it. If you don't, Ask For Help.

Commitments

- Say "Protocol Check" as soon as you become aware of the

incorrect use of a protocol, or of a broken Core Commitment. Do this regardless of the current activity.

- Be supportive of anyone using Protocol Check.
- Do not shame or punish anyone using Protocol Check.
- Ask for help as soon as you realize you are unsure of the correct protocol use.

PRACTICE COMMITMENT 1 PART 1: DISCLOSING AND PERCEIVING WANTS: PERSONAL ALIGNMENT AND ASK FOR HELP

Where am I? Who am I?
How did I come to be here?
What is this thing called the world?
How did I come into the world?
Why was I not consulted?
And if I am compelled to take part in it,
Where is the director?
I want to see him.
- Søren Kierkegaard

PERSONAL ALIGNMENT

"To be nobody-but-yourself - in a world which is doing its best, night and day, to make you everybody else - means to fight the hardest battle which any human being can fight; and never stop fighting."
- e.e. cummings

At the beginning of the book we said that the most important person in any team is "I". It's each person's clarity about what they want, feel and think and their ability to rationally disclose those three things to others that casts the first strand of the web of me-you connections that make a team.

The first step is for me to know what I want.

But what *do* I want? I'm surrounded by people - marketing companies, family members, "experts", and partners - who have an agenda for me that will fulfill their own wants, but often not my own. In that swirling, constant noise of conflicting messages, hearing the signal of my own message to myself can be hard.

It's often in the sleepless hours, as I turn on the rotisserie of insomnia, that I debate what I want. Security or adventure? Companionship or solitude? Friends and family or introspection? Challenge or ease? Variety or simplicity?

Do I want those things now, but not later? Do I want one thing now, and something else tomorrow? Do I want one thing at work, and something different at home? And do I want work and home to be separate, or integrated?

When I go back into the noisy world, that small voice feeds every decision I make. Consciously or unconsciously, I evaluate every single interaction, idea, possibility and challenge against my current, internal list of wants.

Isn't thinking about what we want selfish? There are those who insist we should stop thinking about what we want and think of others. But even the extraordinary people who devote their lives to helping others know what they want, and live that vision every day. They listen to the voice inside them, and let that internal voice drown out all the other voices trying to pull them away from their vision of service. Knowing what we want is the first step to being coherent in the world, regardless of our purpose.

How do we find what we want? First, we look for the things we love to do, and will do without resistance or a feeling of effort.

Any of us is more likely to voluntarily do what we care about than what bores us, or is simply a duty. Those things I do because I'm expected to, or paid to, or nagged to are what Paul and I call, "checking off the checkboxes." Unless we have intentionally aligned our actions to our wants, we spend most of our time doing our duty, doing what others want us to do, "checking off checkboxes." When we check off the checkboxes, the work gets done, but it is empty, lifeless and sometimes tinged with projected guilt. External motivation – salary, benefits, thanks, and pats on the back – might work for a while, but don't sustain a life of meaning.

There are other things we do, both at work and outside work that are driven by what we want. These are things we will voluntarily do, knowing no one else knows or cares. We'll get them done in terrible weather, with little sleep, or with people we don't like and who challenge our patience. We are driven by our own internal motivation to work on them. Everything else will just have to wait.

We hide our wants from ourselves because we've been taught to think of others instead of ourselves. But the truth will come out. When "checking off the checkboxes" meets what we really want, we are surprised by the struggle that ensues. We convince ourselves we want one thing, but our actions point to the truth.

Niko says he wants to spend more time with his family, but he stays late at work six days a week. Fatima says she wants a close relationship, but she quickly gets bored and distant with everyone she becomes intimate with. Inge says she wants to get fit, but she lets other people's emergencies at work stop her from eating well and getting to the gym. They are getting what they want; they just don't want to know that's what they want. As Jim and Michele McCarthy say, if you don't like what you get, change what you want.

What do you want? If you tell yourself the truth, what surprises do you find? Do you want the job you're in? The relationship you're in? The place where you live?

Do you want to work with those people? To work alone?

Do you want to move more? Sit still more?

Do you want more or less routine?

What kind of life do you want? Who do you want to live with? Work with? What is your purpose here?

But more immediately, what do you want to change today? What have you been tolerating? Whose presence in your life do you want more of? Less of?

The Core Protocol Personal Alignment is the best way to fulfill the commitment of knowing what you want. Take the opportunity to set it down in writing, and support yourself getting it, with some structure and help. When you know and pursue what you want, you'll make a lot more sense to the people around you. That will make it easier for them to trust you enough to close the gap.

Once you know what you want, ask yourself why you don't already have it? What's blocking you? Then ask what virtue would shatter that block into pieces. Is the block Fear? Lack of knowledge? Lack of help? Something else?

What will it take to break through those blocks? Courage? Self-awareness? Integrity? Something else? If you use that virtue to break that block, is there anything else in the way of getting what you want right now? If so, keep working through the steps, digging deeper and deeper.

If not, it's time to make a crucial shift.

Instead of wanting the original outcome, the original list of things you want, shift to wanting the virtue that will get you that outcome.

Realizing that the virtue you work on can get you what you want, the key is then to want the virtue more than the outcome. Put a laser focus on that virtue and make it your touch stone in all decisions about what to do, who to work with, what to work on, when to rest, and when to play.

Wanting the virtue makes it almost guaranteed you will get that virtue, and, by extension and almost incidentally, what you originally wanted. Of course, the possibility that you will get much more than you originally wanted is very high, and your wants and their achievement often become more real, detailed and rich as you build the virtue in yourself.

You wanted a closer relationship? The block was fear? The virtue that would shatter that block, for you, was to believe in yourself? OK, now instead of wanting a closer relationship, switch to wanting the virtue of believing in yourself.

That switch makes all the difference. In fact, it means you will apply believing in yourself to every relationship, particularly with yourself. The closer relationship you originally wanted will happen, and will be just one outcome of a bounty of evidence that you believed in yourself. That virtue becomes what the Core calls your Personal Alignment.

So how does all of this get us to closing the me-you gap? We begin to close the gap when we ask others to help us with our Personal Alignment. When I choose an Alignment virtue, I ask others to use the Investigate Protocol with me. I ask them to ask me open ended questions about my Alignment, why I chose it, and what my goals or evidence will be that I've done what I want to do.

When others ask me questions arising from their curiosity about me, I open up to what I already know about myself but have forgotten. I am also exposed to questions or considerations I could never have thought of myself because I needed another mind to combine with mine to create a new idea. And as I learn about myself, you learn about me at the same time. If I ask you about your Alignment, we both learn.

Try taking the Personal Alignment protocol, as a start, to someone you enjoy spending time with and ask them to Investigate you about your virtue, what's blocking you, and what evidence you'd like to have.

Keep asking people to ask you these questions. Keep thinking about them questions and your answers. Go through the protocol and keep connecting.

When you're ready, ask others the same questions I've suggested for you. Maybe someone along the way has asked you a particularly juicy question that sparked an amazing insight for you and you want to ask someone else the same question. The lovely part about this work is the fascinating revelation of another self in front of our eyes. What was once a human body containing a collection of hidden motivations, habits, ideas, biases, experiences and assumptions begins to open up before us. We close the gap a little.

We all know all this self-reflection and talking to each other is going to take time and energy. Is the return really enough to justify the work? How is this going to help the team or the organization when time is tight already and we're fighting fires every day?

First, the greatest source of wasted time in any organization or in any team is apathy. We check off the checkboxes and keep ourselves at a distance from the people around us. Fear stops us. Self-protection and ego respond to that fear of the unknown with the need for separation, safety, and control. We become zombies, half present and going through the motions.

But if we make a deliberate practice of asking about each other and what we want, and when we share and strengthen our knowledge about what each person wants and our commitment to each other to support achievement of those wants, apathy vanishes. We become important to each other's internal motivation.

Second, I bring my virtue to the team and it becomes part of the environment. If I want courage, and I work on that continually, I bring my learning and discoveries about courage to the team, and the team begins to behave with courage by association.

Each of us putting our best and complete selves into the things we actually care about means when we meet each other, and begin to work together, closing the me-you gap, we know that the person in front of us is authentically present and engaged in the work at hand. They are not zombies, doing what they're told, waiting for their escape.

And we know we won't have to carry zombies along on our own energy and passion until we can escape, or retire, or win the lottery. In fact, we don't have to escape or retire or win the lottery at all, because we're already doing what is best for us.

Gandhi said, "Be the change you want to see." It is a call to bring the best self into action to create the reality the self wants. If you want peace, you must be peaceful. If you want beauty, you must be beautiful, if you want the world to embrace something new, you must be the one to take the first step into the unknown.

Who you are in a group - every nuance, breath, word, and choice – becomes part of what that group, and its products, will become. The individuals and their experiences are the building blocks of the group, and become the characteristics of any product that group creates together. It might be software, a community, a company, or a family.

But every contribution by every person is brick, mortar, nails, and wood in the product. And when each of us brings our personal wants and virtues to closing the me-you gap, we banish apathy.

Together, mutually supportive, we blaze a unique trail no one else can duplicate with every choice we make, and the team and organization reaps a return on investment of many times the original investment spent on us.

Simple Tool: Personal Alignment Protocol

The Personal Alignment protocol helps you penetrate deeply into your desires and find what's blocking you from getting what you want. Use it to discover, articulate, and achieve what you want. The quality of your alignment will be equal to the quality of your results.

Steps

1. Want. Answer the question: "What specifically do I want?"
2. Block. Ask yourself, "What is blocking me from having what I want?"
3. Virtue. Figure out what would remove this block by asking yourself "What virtue--if I had it-- would shatter this block of mine?"
4. Shift. Pretend the virtue you identified is actually what you want.
5. Again. Repeat steps 2 to 4 until this process consistently yields a virtue that is powerful enough to shatter your blocks and get you what you originally thought you wanted.
6. Done. Now write down a personal alignment statement in the form "I want [virtue]." For example, "I want courage."

7. Signal/Response/Assignment. Create a signal to let others know when you are practicing your alignment, and provide a response they can give you to demonstrate support. For example, "When I say/do 'X,' will you say/do 'Y'?" Optionally, turn it into an assignment by saying you will do X a certain number of times per day, where X equals an activity that requires you to practice living your alignment.
8. Evidence. Write, in specific and measurable terms, the long-term evidence of practicing this alignment.
9. Help. Ask each member of your group for help. They help by giving the response you would like when you give your signal that you are practicing your alignment.

Commitments

- Identify an alignment that will result in your personal change and require no change from any other person.
- Identify blocks and wants that are specific and personal.
- Identify blocks that, if solved, would radically increase your effectiveness in life, work, and play.
- Choose a virtue that is about you and preferably one word long. For example: integrity, passion, self-care, peace, fun.
- Ask for help from people who know you and/or know alignments.
- Identify evidence that is measurable by an objective third party.

Notes

- The most popular personal alignments are "I want (Integrity, Courage, Passion, Peace, Self-Awareness or Self-Care)".
- If you are struggling with figuring out what you want, adopt the alignment "I want self-awareness." There is no case where increased self-awareness would not be beneficial.
- A personal block is something you find within yourself. It does not refer to circumstances or other people. Assume that you could have had what you want by now, that your block is a myth that somehow deprives you of your full potential.
- Ideally, identify both immediate and long-term evidence of your alignment. Write down results that start now (or very soon), as well as results you'll see at least five or more years in the future.
- As a default signal, tell your teammates or others who are

close to you that you are working on your alignment when you are practicing it. If they don't know the protocol, just tell them what virtue you are working on and ask for their help.

- When members of a team are completing their personal alignments together (asking each other for help), the final step of the process is most powerful if done as a ceremony.

ASK FOR HELP

It is not the answer that enlightens but the question.
- Eugene Ionesco

At the beginning of the journey to close the me-you gap, we talked about the first Commitment, to *know and disclose* what we want. Personal Alignment helps us *know* what we want.

Ask For Help is one of the Protocols that help us *disclose* what we want by making ourselves and what we want transparent to others. And it helps us close the gap with them as they help us. The second major Core Commitment was to always seek effective help. Combining the first two commitments, Ask For Help gets us a long way in the journey.

In my experience as a Core Instructor, with many teams, many camps and hundreds of people, this is the most powerful, and most effective commitment for closing the me-you gap, the commitment that looks the easiest, but paradoxically, is the commitment people ignore and try to avoid for the longest time. Having a great tool to get past all of our cultural biases about asking for help helps us keep that commitment and reap all the great connection and success that comes with asking for help.

Some of us are endowed with an easy grace when it comes to asking for help. But, I have seen that, for many of the rest of us, asking for help is a fearsome act.

We are loaded with fears: fear of looking stupid, needy, incompetent, junior, unworthy, fear of being in debt to another, fear of being rejected, being scorned, made fun of, criticized, shamed, teased. We have all kinds of self-imposed reasons to avoid asking for help. And the really deep reason we don't ask is that we will feel uncomfortable when we ask.

If you're like me, from the moment you entered school, your education taught you to go solo, to win the prize by being the smartest, to compete, to be the "best". Then you wrote up your resume, noting all of the things you accomplished all on your own, and you got a job based on your personal competencies, your ability to get things done without a lot of help from others.

And now I'm telling you to Ask For Help.

Yes. Not only that, but I'm suggesting that you Ask For Help when you know you need it, *and* when you think you don't need it, *and* even when you don't want to ask.

I suggest you ask people you know, people you don't know, people who can help, people who you aren't sure can help, and people who you know can't. If that sounds like a lot of asking for help, you've got the picture.

How do you know that someone might be able to help? We usually ask people who have helped other people we know, or they've helped us in the past.

Yes, past evidence is one way to evaluate the potential for help. We ask because they're experts in what we need help with. If you're asking for help with the technical aspects of brain surgery, it makes sense to go to a person with expertise in brain surgery.

But here's the key with Ask For Help. It's usually the people who aren't the acknowledged "experts" who truly connect with us when we ask. An experts' job is to give answers about their subject. If that's what you're after, perfect. But once an expert is finished giving their answer (getting what they want, by the way), they're finished with you.

Anyone else who responds to an Ask For Help is answering because of some other reason, often the chance to connect with you. Since it's the connection that matters, not the answer, don't be too concerned about whether someone can help or not. Remember, we're trying to close the me-you gap. We're not trying to do brain surgery.

And we might get lucky and get both connection and some great help. As I said at the beginning, everyone is hidden from us. The help we're looking for could be waiting inside the head of the very person we pass on the street every day with whom we never even make eye contact. It's not until we close the me-you gap that we learn what they know.

You're sitting with a colleague and the conversation has waned. You're trying to find something to talk about so you mentioned a problem you've been struggling with for weeks. And the person you were with said something like, "Oh, ya. That happened to me too. I fixed it by..." And just like that, the solution falls in your lap.

Or you are sitting around the table with acquaintances who are all art directors, and they ask you about your engineering project. You think to yourself, "I'd better keep this at a high level." So you start describing the project, and one of them asks you some very specific technical questions that hit right at the heart of the work you're doing.

You are suddenly awake. You ask how he knows about engineering. It turns out his wife is an engineer working on some very similar projects. He's heard all about them over dinner and his questions, combining his perspective on both engineering and art direction have raised some new possibilities you'd never considered. Now you will make sure to connect with him and his wife at the next opportunity.

And then there's my favourite: you're frustrated about a problem. You wander into the kitchen, and your eleven-year-old is eating toast at the kitchen table. She asks what's wrong. You start to explain the problem, and between bites of peanut butter and jam she asks some simple questions. *Boom!* There's the answer. It's been in your head all along, and all you needed was someone, anyone, to provide some structure for you to think about it out loud.

For technical problems with technical solutions, it's admittedly helpful to get help from someone who knows the technical environment. But simply thinking differently about problems can reveal potential solutions. We get different thinking by bringing another, different, head to the problem. In those cases it almost doesn't matter who you Ask For Help. Bringing non-technical thinking to it can shift even a technical problem. Making our boundaries a little more permeable can get us unstuck, and close the me-you gap at the same time.

What happens when someone says, "No"? That's fine. Just find someone else to ask.

And what happens when someone asks you for help and you want to say, "No"? Well, as the protocol says, just say, "no." Remember we're after authentic, aligned, rational, coherent, behaviour that's reliable and consistent. Saying, "yes" when you want to say, "no" isn't any of those things.

The person being asked has the responsibility to say, "no." That means you don't have to wait until you think they're ready, or be concerned about interrupting them. They will say, "no" if they want to, and if they don't, that means they want to help. They're grown up. They can look after themselves.

In general people Ask For Help much less frequently than helpers are willing to offer help. Go ahead. I dare you to try asking for too much help. I bet you can't. And I bet that, in the process, you'll close a lot of gaps.

Simple Tool: Ask For Help Protocol

The Ask For Help protocol allows you to efficiently make use of the skills and knowledge of others. Ask For Help is the act that catalyzes connection and shared vision. Use it continuously, before and during the pursuit of any result.

Steps

1. Asker inquires of another, "[Helper's name], will you X?"
2. Asker expresses any specifics or restrictions of the request.
3. Helper responds by saying "Yes" or "No" or by offering an alternative form of help.

Commitments

- Always invoke the Ask For Help Protocol with the phrase "Will you . . .
- Have a clear understanding of what you want from the Helper or if you do not have a clear understanding of what help you want, signal this by saying "I'm not sure what I need help with, but will you help me?"
- Assume that all Helpers are always available and trust that any Helper accepts the responsibility to say "No."
- Say "No" any time you do not want to help.
- Accept the answer "No" without any inquiry or emotional drama.
- Be receptive of the help offered.
- Offer your best help even if it is not what the asker is expecting.
- Postpone the help request if you are unable to fully engage.
- Request more information if you are unclear about the specifics of the help request.
- Do not apologize for asking for help.

Notes

- Asking for help is a low-cost undertaking. The worst possible outcome is a "No," which leaves you no further ahead or behind than when you asked. In the best possible outcome, you reduce the amount of time required to achieve a task and/or learn.
- Helpers should say "No" if they are not sure if they want to help. They should say nothing else after turning down a request for help.
- You cannot "over-ask" a given person for help unless he or she has asked you to respect a particular limit.
- If you don't understand the value of what is offered, or feel that it wouldn't be useful, or believe yourself to have considered and rejected the idea offered previously, assume a curious stance instead of executing a knee-jerk "But . . ."

rejection. (See the Investigate protocol.)

- Asking in time of trouble means you waited too long to Ask For Help. Ask for help when you are doing well.
- Simply connecting with someone, even if he or she knows nothing of the subject you need help on can help you find answers within yourself, especially if you ask that person to Investigate you.

PRACTICE COMMITMENT 1 PART 2: DISCLOSING AND PERCEIVING THOUGHTS: INVESTIGATE, PERFECTION GAME AND DECIDER/RESOLUTION

I don't like that man. I must get to know him better.
- Abraham Lincoln

INVESTIGATE

*Listening is a magnetic and strange thing, a creative force. The friends who
listen to us are the ones we move toward. When we are listened to,
it creates us, makes us unfold and expand.*
- Shel Silverstein

Investigate helps fulfill the Commitment to seek to perceive more than be
perceived and it's a safe, simple, powerful tool for learning more about others
and closing the gap.

Most of us go through our lives fighting to be heard. We build up some
very effective defenses against being ignored, criticized and invalidated.

The problem with those defenses is they can get in our way. We start to
fear that if we listen to someone else too much they'll dominate the
conversation and we'll never get heard.

Or we really want to know about others, but we've been taught awkward,
mechanical, conversation techniques that feel more like manipulation than
heartfelt connection.

We talk about ourselves in the wrong contexts, and don't have mutual
agreements about when it's ok to be open and when we need to be
circumspect. Investigate makes the potentially complex activity of disclosing
and perceiving, simple and effective.

Investigate is intentional curiosity about another human being. The
following sums it up: be curious, let go of agendas and judgment, ask
questions that you want to ask, and keep asking until you're satisfied.

If your friend does something that seems strange, like spends time with
people who deliberately hurt her, you could say, "Will you let me Investigate
you about your friends?" If she says yes, you could ask questions like, "You've

said they hurt you and you still spend time with them. Will you tell me what is attractive about them for you?"

If your colleague appears to have a particular approach that seems different than the one you use, try asking, "Will you tell me what you like about that approach?"

And if your partner or spouse is behaving differently, ask, "I'm curious what's different for you lately. Will you tell me?"

It's important for everyone involved in Investigate, or any interaction for that matter, to know they can use the Safety Protocol Pass on answering any question, any time. That's what the safety gear is for; Pass, Check Out, Intention Check, and Protocol Check are all tools we can use when someone Investigates us. Safety is, again, at the root of trust and intimacy.

If you're Investigating, you can help keep the safety high. For every question you ask, first ask yourself what your intent is. Are you curious, a fundamentally good thing in any me-you gap work? Or do you have a hidden agenda, which will keep the gap wide open?

In general the best questions are open-ended and start with "What?"

"What is important to you about...?"

"What would be the best outcome for you if...?"

"What are you excited about...?"

"What happens when...?"

If you think you're asking a leading question, ask it a different way, a way that leaves open the possibility of an answer you weren't expecting. Instead of "Don't you think it would be better if...?" ask, "What would happen if...?"

Stay away from questions that result in yes/no. Sometimes you need to ask those to get context, but yes/no questions tend to sound like you're in the interrogation room at the local police office and that's not where the juicy me-you gap-closing connection is.

Questions that start with "Why?" almost always backfire. They sound accusatory, like your mother. "Why do you spend time with those people?" sounds like a rephrase of "I can't understand why someone as smart as you spends time with people like that." Even if you didn't mean the question like that, that's how it's likely to be heard, so just put "Why?" into a box in the back of the closet and forget about it.

Investigate can heal many hurts. A friend of mine was struggling with her father. They had been close many years ago, but as he got older and she made life choices he didn't think were helpful for her, they stopped talking. One day he called her and told her he had cancer. So she thought hard about what she wanted for both of them and decided it was to become close again.

She drove across the country to see him and as she walked in to his room and she saw him, frail, weak and hooked up to several machines, she decided she had no words. She realized everything he knew and had done and all the people he had known and all the stories he could share were all going to be gone. Everything she had meant to say left her in that moment. So she sat down beside him and just asked him questions. And slowly, story-by-story, she learned who this man was whom she had been shunning for twenty years. She learned about his love of medieval history, that he enjoyed cooking Thai food, that he had been playing lead roles in the local theatre productions of Shakespeare plays. She found out that he had been writing a book about their family and was nearly finished.

She began bringing copies of Shakespeare plays to the hospital and reading the other parts as he took the lead role. They spent hours together and she saw what a sparkling, charming and talented man he was. Her memory of him as the tyrannical, mean-hearted, humourless, old-fashioned authority figure was being overwritten by new memories. When he died, she finished his book and took season's tickets to the theatre. Of course, inevitably she regretted having lost the time she could have spent with him. But that wasn't the only thing she had left of him.

Learning about someone else starts with *wanting* to learn about them. Wanting to have a glimpse inside the gallery of their memories, thoughts, feelings and experiences. One of my favourite questions to ask someone is, "What's the most interesting place you've ever been?" I've had answers like "a clothing factory in Guangdong province, China," from a corporate IT sales guy and "My wife's village in Pakistan," from a courier in rural Nova Scotia, and "Antarctica," from the checkout clerk at the grocery store. People are fascinating! There is just no knowing what's behind their skin.

What memories does this executive have of being a peacekeeper in Egypt thirty years ago before starting his corporate career? Or this stay-at-home mom of prospecting for diamonds? Or that project manager of working for his parents in a chick hatching operation? Or that developer of being a studio potter before going back to school?

Wanting to hear their story, know their way of seeing and interacting with the world, exploring their complexity and beauty and glory is what closing the me-you gap is all about. Finding out about another's journey teaches us options for ourselves. It's an example of thriving despite swimming against the wisdom of the crowd. And the more we see each other as complex, multidimensional points of light in a spectrum of possibility, the more flexibility we have in our interactions with each other.

When I decide to learn about someone, I always feel a little afraid. What if I find out something I would rather not know? What if my view of the world is completely changed by their story? What if I get caught up in their drama? It's uncomfortable to really open up to the possibility of another person's reality

That fear is old thinking talking to the me in the present experience. Learning from others doesn't necessarily mean joining their cause, doing their work, or buying their book. I can learn about them and their place in the world and how they got here, and that alone is valuable to me. With the safety protocols, I can be open to new ideas without having to endorse them. If I choose to I can go deeper. And if they choose to they can respond.

And that's another good reason to know yourself before asking about others, something the Personal Alignment Protocol can support. When I'm aligned, I won't be overwhelmed by who you are. I don't need to endorse you to acknowledge you. I can be with you, witness your truth, and have my own truth at the same time.

It's also scary to learn about someone else if we believe that learning about one another will lead to an unwanted obligation to support. Some folks are happy to share a lot very quickly and to be very transparent and unfiltered. Others prefer to limit the emotional input they get from others because it can be too overwhelming.

The safety inherent in the Core Protocols and Commitments helps avoid the "stickiness" we can sometimes sense when learning about one another. Investigate is a neutral way of sharing ourselves that maintains both our freedoms. I can be me, authentically, genuinely me, and still close the gap with you.

Simple Tool: Investigate Protocol

Investigate allows you to learn about a phenomenon that occurs in someone else. Use it when an idea or behavior someone is presenting seems poor, confusing, or simply interesting.

Steps

1. Act as if you were a detached but fascinated inquirer, asking questions until your curiosity is satisfied or you no longer want to ask questions.

Commitments

- Ask well-formed questions.
- Ask only questions that will increase your understanding.
- Ask questions only if the subject is engaged and appears ready to answer more.
- Refrain from offering opinions.
- Do not ask leading questions where you think you know how he or she will answer.
- If you cannot remain a detached, curious investigator with no agenda, stop using the protocol until you can come back to it and keep these commitments.

Notes

- Do not theorize about the subject or provide any sort of diagnosis.
- Consider using the following forms for your questions:
  o What about X makes you Y Z?
  o Would you explain a specific example?
  o How does X go when it happens?
  o What is the one thing you want most from solving X?
  o What is the biggest problem you see regarding X now?
  o What is the most important thing you could do right now to help you with X?
- Ineffective queries include the following:
  o Questions that lead or reflect an agenda.
  o Questions that attempt to hide an answer you believe is true.
  o Questions that invite stories.
  o Questions that begin with "Why."
- Stick to your intention of gathering more information.
- If you feel that you will explode if you can't say what's on your mind, you shouldn't speak at all. Consider checking your intention or Check Out.

PERFECTION GAME

At school, new ideas are thrust at you every day. Out in the world, you'll have
to find your inner motivation to seek for new ideas on your own.
- Bill Watterson

Perfection Game is a tool that helps with a few of the Commitments: asking
for effective help, seeking the improvement of an idea, and using teams to do
difficult things. It also helps us perceive and disclose thoughts, part of our
first commitment. And it's a really fun way to close the me-you gap.

Asking others for their ideas in a way that creates fun and safety for you
both adds extra value to your connection. People love to give ideas. And we
can get some genuinely great ideas if we invite them - the best, most amazing
ideas the other person has.

Perfection Game invites another person to share what they like about
something and to give their ideas for making it ten out of ten; literally, perfect
for them. It's a brilliant way to get ideas out of others' heads without falling
into the unsolicited feedback and "I don't like" traps.

It's a no-risk, high return conversation for both sides. There's no
obligation to do what's suggested, so the wildest ideas can see the light of day
without being filtered for practicality. Because we're aiming for something
impossible - absolute perfection - we can think of and share some really big,
outrageous ideas. And not only do I get your ideas, I get a glimpse of how
you think, what matters to you, and we get a chance to come together in a
meeting of the minds that closes the me-you gap.

Perfection Game is fun. If I have ideas to give you, I do. If you want to
use them, you do. In the meantime, we can laugh, share crazy ideas, and open
up our minds a lot more than we usually do in a world mostly centred on next
month's results. In either case, we know a little, or a lot, more about one
another and how we think,

It's a safe way to dream together. There is no judgment, criticism, or coercion in Perfection Game. And you don't need to know what I don't like; we can skip past that time-waster and get straight to what we can take action on. I will tell you what to keep from the original and what new ideas I have for you. And when I'm done, you don't have to argue, defend, explain or try to change my mind. You can simply say "Thank you."

Perfection Game is a great tool to use at work. Instead of asking for "feedback" which often descends into "I don't like" territory with no solutions or improvements offered, ask the other person to "Perfect" what you're doing or thinking.

Got to deliver a presentation? Ask your colleague to tell you what he likes about it and what would make it perfect for him. Want to know what the boss thinks of your performance? Ask her to tell you what she likes and what would make you the perfect employee. Going to a customer meeting? Ask your customer what she loves about your service, and what would make it a ten for her. Close those gaps!

And each interaction gives you more than just new ideas. It creates a land bridge of value between two isolated minds. You get to see what is important and interesting to me. And I get to see you gracefully seek and receive new ideas. You inspire me to try Perfection Game myself and to be open to the ideas of others, and I give you a different way of looking at a problem and a chance to practice closing the gap.

And we get that little bit closer.

Simple Tool: Perfection Game Protocol

The Perfection Game protocol will support you in your desire to aggregate the best ideas. Use it whenever you desire to improve something you've created.

Steps

1. Perfectee performs an act or presents an object for perfection, optionally saying "Begin" and "End" to notify the Perfector of the start and end of the performance.
2. Perfector rates the value of the performance or object on a scale of 1 to 10 based on how much value the Perfector believes he or she can add.
3. Perfector says, "What I liked about the performance or object was X," and proceeds to list the qualities of the object the Perfector thought were of high quality or should be amplified.
4. Perfector offers the improvements to the performance or object required for it to be rated a 10 by saying "To make it a

ten, you would have to do X."

Commitments

- Accept perfecting without argument.
- Give only positive comments: what you like and what it would take to "give it a 10."
- Abstain from mentioning what you don't like or being negative in other ways.
- Withhold points only if you can think of improvements.
- Use ratings that reflect a scale of improvement rather than a scale of how much you liked the object.
- If you cannot say something you liked about the object or specifically say how to make the object better, you must give it a 10.

Notes

- A rating of 10 means you are unable to add value, and a rating of 5 means you will specifically describe how to make the object at least twice as good.
- The important information to transmit in the Perfection Game protocol improves the performance or object. For example, "The ideal sound of a finger snap for me is one that is crisp, has sufficient volume, and startles me somewhat. To get a 10, you would have to increase your crispness."

As a perfectee, you may only ask questions to clarify or gather more information for improvement. If you disagree with the ideas given to you, simply don't include them.

DECIDER AND RESOLUTION

Honest disagreement is often a good sign of progress.
- Mohandas K. Gandhi

Another way to disclose what we think in a results-oriented way is to make decisions and resolve disagreements. If achieving our ideas affects others, The Decider and Resolver Protocols are a way to quickly disclose those ideas and perceive the support we have from others to turn the ideas into action.

I start with knowing what I want and what I think: what do I want from this project and what do I think about the choice the project manager made? What do I want from working with this team and what do I think the team should do next? What do I want from the next few weeks of work and what do I think the best approach is to completing the next milestone?

Knowing what I want and think means that when I need to make a decision or choose between alternatives, I won't lie to myself about the outcome or the risks. I'll make a coherent decision that I'm willing to support, offer my best help when I'm asked, know when to check the intent of another, or simply know what I should do next, even if that means doing something that is temporarily unpleasant or uncomfortable.

If I know my own thoughts well enough that I can bring thoughts and actions and words into alignment I can be coherent in my relationships with my teammates. The Decider Protocol helps us clearly share what we think so our thoughts can be quickly evaluated, improved and if accepted can become actions. Making clear proposals, and being committed to their achievement if they are unanimously accepted, is a clean way of closing the me-you gap on thoughts. If I agree, I'll support you. If I have a better idea, I can resolve the difference with you cleanly.

Here's what happens when we don't share thoughts effectively:

Ann and Doug are fighting again.

"You didn't tell me you were going to change the plan."

"It slipped my mind and you've been so busy there was no time to talk about it."

"You always do this."

"Do what?"

"Make these unilateral decisions and then pretend it's my fault you didn't involve me."

"I don't 'always' do that. You're just overreacting."

"Well you don't need me to be involved even though I'm affected by this. I don't promise to go along with it if I think it's not working, you know."

"Fine, you decide. If you want all the control, you make the decision and just do the work yourself."

"No, I want us both to have input."

"If we both have input we'll never make a decision!"

You know this could go on and on. It doesn't matter who plays Ann and who plays Doug, or whether they're at work, at home, or on a volunteer committee. This is the kind of conflict that gives conflict a bad name. When smarts meet integrity, there's often conflict. We come from different backgrounds with different experiences, and often when we close the gap, the arising thoughts are in conflict.

Entire consultancies exist to help people learn to deal with decisions and conflict. I'll share the secret they want you to pay them buckets of money to learn. Ready? Here it is:

You have to *get unanimity* AND *want to resolve* disagreements.

First, get unanimity:

If I have a great idea, I propose it for your vote. If you love it we don't have to talk about it any more – we have to get into action. Let's go!

If you don't love it, but don't have a better idea, and you're not absolutely opposed to it, you agree to actively support me working toward it until we think of something better. Again we get right into action without further discussion.

If you have a better idea, tell me what it is. If I'm not absolutely opposed to it, I'll actively support you until we think of something better. Ideas are like trains: the next one will be along any minute. Again, the next step is action. Getting the idea?

So far, we've kept supporting the best idea by taking action to make it happen. It's going with the best idea until a better one arises (remember the Commitment to do just that?).

What we haven't done is keep talking after agreeing to the original idea, modifying the idea with each person's input until it's so confused and watered down that it's so unrecognizable, so incoherent, and so uninspiring we don't want to, nor do we know how to, take action on it.

We also haven't forced anyone to take action they were opposed to. Never, ever force an idea on someone else or "just go along with" another person's idea. If is the majority of people are lukewarm on an idea or actively opposed, it's unlikely they will warm up as the work begins. You might think that your passion will carry both of you forward, but the likely outcome is that you will be resentful, they will be unhappy and undermine the work in revenge, and you'll end up dropping the idea after you've put some good energy and time into it.

If this happens, it's in indication the gap is opening up. Before working any more, stop, Investigate each other, and seek to perceive each other's wants. A better idea will emerge from that discussion that will be much more powerful useful and sustainable for you both than dragging along the dead horse of an idea neither of you is passionate about.

If you find yourself in the even worse situation of falling into fighting, arguing about details or blaming each other for lack of results, something has gone very wrong, and it's time to put all your focus on the gap. Move into resolution.

When you're disagreeing, you have to decide that getting resolution is better than not getting resolution. If you're in the middle of a Decider, follow the Resolution Protocol to the letter. It works like a charm.

But if you're experiencing conflict outside of a Decider, use this modified version, which Michele McCarthy taught me. When you decide that you want resolution, you say, "I want to resolve this. Do you?" And wait for the answer. If it's "yes", say, "What will it take for this to be resolved for you?" Wait for the answer. Say if you're willing to do that or if you'd be willing to do something else. Then say, "This is what it would take for it to be resolved for me. Will you do that?" And wait for the answer.

Then ask each other for help to take action on the answers. The key is to stay with the intention of resolution, and not get emotionally caught up in being right, or being validated, or getting empathy. There's no guarantee you'll get any of those things, but if you work at it you will get resolution and you can both move forward. It's hard on our egos sometimes, but it's worth it to close the gap, because resolution leads to more resolution, fewer endless fights, and more trust. And the fewer ultimate stands we take, the more the stands we take get noticed and attended to. So save up your stands for the things that really matter to you.

Let's say Doug asks Ann what it would take to resolve their argument, and Ann says, "What it will take is for me to know you'll tell me if you're going to change the plan we made."

Doug says, "Will you help me figure out how to do that if I can't reach you but I need to make a decision right away?"

Ann says, "Leave me a voice mail with the details and what the new plan is. Then I know the plan has changed and I'm not surprised."

Then Ann asks Doug what it will take to resolve their disagreement. Doug says, "I want us to not use absolutes like "never" and "always" when we talk about each other. Let's try to be more precise so we can keep moving forward."

Then they both have to look after getting what they want out of the agreement. If Doug misses telling Ann about the plan, she can say, "Doug, we agreed you would leave me a voicemail about a change in plan. You didn't do that this time. What happened? And what will be different next time?"

And Doug can help Ann in the middle of a conversation if she falls back on absolutes by saying, "Ann, we agreed we wouldn't use "always" and "never". What happened? And what will be different next time?"

It's really easy to slip back into argument mode, so if you're sure you can't be rational about resolution, Check Out for a while so you don't make things worse.

When I know you'll resolve a disagreement, I'll be much more likely to want to spend time with you, work with you and count on you. You'll have closed the gap a little with me.

Simple Tool: Decider Protocol; Resolution Protocol

Decider

Use Decider anytime you want to move a group immediately and unanimously towards results.

Steps

1. Proposer says, "I propose [concise, actionable behavior]."
2. Proposer says "1-2-3."
3. Voters, using either Yes (thumbs up), No (thumbs down), or Support-it (flat hand), vote simultaneously with other voters.
4. Voters who absolutely cannot get in on the proposal declare themselves by saying "I am an absolute no. I won't get in." If this occurs, the proposal is withdrawn.
5. Proposer counts the votes.
6. Proposer withdraws the proposal if a combination of outliers (No votes) and Support-it votes is too great or if proposer expects not to successfully conclude Resolution (below). You can approximate "too great" by using the following heuristics:
   - approximately 50% (or greater) of votes are Support-it, OR
   - the anticipated gain if the proposal Passes is less than the likely cost of Resolution effort

7. Proposer uses the **Resolution** protocol with each outlier to bring him in by asking, "What will it take to get you in?"
8. Proposer declares the proposal carried if all outliers change their votes to Yes or Support-it.
9. The team is now committed to the proposed result.

Commitments

- Propose no more than one item per proposal.
- Remain present until the Decider protocol is complete; always remain aware of how your behavior either moves the group forward or slows it down.
- Give your full attention to a proposal over and above all other activity.
- Speak only when you are the proposer or are directed to speak by the proposer.
- Keep the reasons you voted as you did to yourself during the protocol.
- Reveal immediately when you are an absolute no voter and be ready to propose a better idea.
- Be personally accountable for achieving the results of a Decider commitment even if it was made in your absence.
- Keep informed about Decider commitments made in your absence.
- Do not argue with an absolute no voter. Always ask him or her for a better idea.
- Actively support the decisions reached.
- Use your capacity to "stop the show" by declaring you "won't get in no matter what" with great discretion and as infrequently as possible.
- Insist at all times that the Decider and **Resolution** protocols be followed exactly as per specification, regardless of how many times you find yourself doing the insisting.
- Do not Pass during a Decider.
- Unceasingly work toward forward momentum; have a bias toward action.
- Do not look at how others are voting to choose your own vote.
- Avoid using Decider in large groups. Break up into small subgroups to make decisions, and use the large group to report status.

Notes

- Vote No only when you really believe the contribution to forward momentum you will make to the group after slowing or stopping it in the current vote will greatly outweigh the (usually considerable) costs you are adding by voting No.
- If you are unsure or confused by a proposal, support it and seek clarification offline after the proposal is resolved. If you have an alternate proposal after receiving more information, you can have faith that your team will support the best idea. (See "The Core Commitments")
- Voting No to make minor improvements to an otherwise acceptable proposal slows momentum and should be avoided. Instead, offer an additional proposal after the current one Passes or, better yet, involve yourself in the implementation to make sure your idea gets in.
- Withdraw weak proposals. If a proposal receives less than seventy percent (approximately) Yes votes, it is a weak proposal and should be withdrawn by the proposer. This decision is, however, at the discretion of the proposer.
- Think of yourself as a potential solo outlier every time you vote No.
- Vote Absolute No only when you are convinced you have a significant contribution to make to the direction or leadership of the group, or when integrity absolutely requires it of you.

Resolution

When a **Decider** vote yields a small minority of outliers, the proposer quickly leads the team, in a highly structured fashion, to deal with the outliers. The Resolution protocol promotes forward momentum by focusing on bringing outliers in at least cost.

Steps

1. Proposer asks outlier "What will it take to get you in?"
2. Outlier states in a single, short, declarative sentence the precise modification required to be in.
3. Proposer offers to adopt the outlier's changes or withdraws the proposal.

Notes

- If the outlier's changes are simple, a simple Eye Check is performed to determine if everyone is still in.
- If the outlier's changes are complex, the proposer must withdraw the current proposal and then submit a new proposal that incorporates the outlier's changes.
- If the outlier begins to say why he voted No or to explain anything other than what it will take to get him in, the proposer must interrupt the outlier with "What will it take to get you in?"

PRACTICE COMMITMENT 1 PART 3:
DISCLOSING AND PERCEIVING FEELINGS:
CHECK IN

Feelings like disappointment, embarrassment, irritation, resentment, anger, jealousy, and fear, instead of being bad news, are actually very clear moments that teach us where it is that we're holding back. They teach us to perk up and lean in when we feel we'd rather collapse and back away. They're like messengers that show us, with terrifying clarity, exactly where we're stuck. This very moment is the perfect teacher, and, lucky for us, it's with us wherever we are.
- Pema Chodron

CHECK IN

Every man has his secret sorrows which the world knows not; and often
times we call a man cold
when he is only sad.
Henry Wadsworth Longfellow

We said in the Commitments that we were going to know and disclose what we want, think and feel. The Protocols Personal Alignment, and Ask For Help, help us know and disclose what we want. Investigate, Perfection Game and Decider/Resolution help us know and disclose what we think.

Now, using Check In, we're going to work on the last part of the first Commitment, knowing and disclosing what we feel. Check In also helps with the Commitment to "decline to offer and refuse to accept incoherent emotional transmissions." When we know and disclose our feelings coherently, we make sense to people and it's easier for them to feel safe with us.

We can tell when others are feeling strongly about something even if they say nothing. Children and animals certainly can tell when we're afraid, angry, glad or sad. So why is it so hard sometimes to discern our own, or others, feelings?

Part of the reason we have a hard time knowing our own feelings is we have learned to suppress feelings when we are around others. Showing emotion in many cultures and families is considered immature, unprofessional or weak. With no effective way to share feelings, we hide them. That also makes it hard to disclose our feelings coherently even if we want to. The people around us may get a very confused message from us, because we ourselves are confused.

But keeping strong feelings hidden takes a lot of energy and focus. It's often easier to hide the feelings from ourselves as well as from others. But all that hiding doesn't stop our behaviour from reflecting our emotion. Feelings will come out whether we suppress them or not. And when we hide them from ourselves and others we all lose the useful information emotion gives us in closing the me-you gap.

If I know I'm angry about a missed deadline, which tells me the deadline was important to me. I can use the energy from the anger to take action so we don't miss another one. If I notice how I feel working with different people, I can seek opportunities to work with the people I enjoy and am successful with. If I'm aware that I'm scared about the project schedule, I can learn more about the work that needs to be done, get help, change some parameters, or talk to the customer about it. And if I'm sad, I can reflect on what I've lost and seek comfort with good friends.

When we aren't aware of our feelings because we've hidden them from even ourselves, we may say and do things that don't make sense to the people around us, and that creates turbulence and distraction in the web of me-you connections. When there's turbulence, people tend to widen the me-you gap. The simpler and easier it is to understand the emotional environment around us, the less we are distracted by others' behaviours and the safer it is to bring our real selves to our connections and work. So if we want to close the me-you gap, we need to know what we feel.

Closing the me-you gap relies on safety and consistency. If I'm angry but refuse to see my own anger, and it comes out as mixed signals of anger, sadness and fear, the people around me will have to spend more time and effort to connect with me I might talk about being sad in an angry voice. I might behave aggressively but tell stories about being fearful. When people are around confused emotions, they become afraid because the signals they're getting don't line up. If I'm behaving angrily but saying I'm fine, they will be afraid of the unknown inside my head. And if I'm confused about how I feel, I won't be able to get what I need to resolve my feelings, and I'll continue to behave unpredictably, clouding the conversations I'm part of.

Have you ever had the sense that your teammate or partner was thinking something but not saying what she thought? Or he feels strongly about something, but is saying everything is fine? What do you do?

If you're like me, the first thing you do is think the worst: it's my fault. I didn't get the report to him on time. I left my socks on the floor. I forgot to fill up on gas. I included someone in the cc: list on the email I shouldn't have.

Another strategy is to think it's someone else's fault. You go through the lists of the mistakes that people have made this week. The botched presentations, the broken lamp, the customer who walked away from the deal.

Closing the me-you gap by being explicit about our feelings helps us all stop wondering and watching. We might even be able to take some action to resolve or comfort the feelings. Whatever we do, we can bias ourselves toward action.

The hard part about sharing feelings is that we worry how other people will react to them. I've had people tell me I shouldn't feel sad or mad or afraid. They give me all kinds of reasons: I need to see the bright side; I don't have to worry; it's not my fault; it's not their fault; I need to be professional; I need to think of others instead of myself; I need to get a thicker skin; and so on. Maybe this has happened to you.

Telling someone not to feel their feelings is like telling them not to taste their food. They can't do what you're asking. Check In combines the best of sharing feelings and being rational. It's about thinking and feeling at the same time. For most of us who have worked in highly emotionally charged workplaces, Check In is a breath of fresh air.

When someone Checks In with you, listen. Then welcome them. And that's it.

You don't have to validate, endorse, solve the problem, and make them feel better, or judge them or anyone else. All you have to do is bear witness to someone disclosing their feelings, and let that information explain their subsequent behaviour. You don't even have to help. They might explicitly ask you to help them with what they've told you, and that's the protocol Ask For Help,.

When you Check In, enjoy the freedom of disclosing how you feel without fear or consequence. You can share your feelings knowing your listener won't be feeling obligated to be your therapist, to empathize, to figure out the solution to the problem you're having, or "make you feel better." And you don't have to deal with being psychoanalyzed, or listening to how *they* dealt with exactly the same problem. You also don't have to deal with the equally awkward problem of your listener becoming so upset by your feelings that now *you* have to make *them* "feel better!"

I used to get angry, something I learned over the years was not well received. I would try to suppress it by saying nothing. Because I was behaving like an angry person but not saying a word about it Paul often worried he was to blame for my mood. The number of times I was angry with him was negligible, but the time he spent being afraid that he had done something wrong was significant.

When I Checked In he could see that he wasn't to blame. Instead of stomping about for days in a righteous rage, I could say, for instance, "I'm angry about the conversation I just had with my customer. The whole project is broken and I know this will end badly. I'm In." And Paul could say, "Welcome," and get on with his day without rescuing me, finding a solution, or tiptoeing around me, worrying about whether or not he had done something to upset me.

Even better, I could combine Check in and Ask For Help, and after I'd checked in I could say, "Will you help me with ideas for how I could fix what's wrong and get this project back on track?" And he could say yes, or no, or something like, "No but I'll help you figure out ways to gracefully get out of the contract. I think it's going to end badly too." And then we could continue to enjoy each other and our amazing connection.

Simple Tool: Check In Protocol

Use Check In to begin meetings or anytime an individual or group Check In would add more value to the current team interactions.

Steps

1. Speaker says "I feel [one or more of MAD, SAD, GLAD, AFRAID]." Speaker may provide a brief explanation. Or if others have already checked in, the speaker may say "I Pass." (See the Pass protocol.)
2. Speaker says "I'm in." This signifies that Speaker intends to behave according to the Core Commitments.
3. Listeners respond, "Welcome."

Commitments

- State feelings without qualification.
- State feelings only as they pertain to yourself.
- Be silent during another's Check In.
- Do not refer to another's Check In disclosures without explicitly granted permission from him or her.

Notes

- In the context of the Core Protocols, all emotions are expressed through combinations of MAD, SAD, GLAD, or AFRAID. For example, "excited" may be a combination of GLAD and AFRAID.
- Check In as deeply as possible. Checking in with two or more emotions is the norm. The depth of a group's Check In translates directly to the quality of the group's results.
- Do not do anything to diminish your emotional state. Do not describe yourself as a "little" mad, sad, glad, or afraid or say "I'm mad, but I'm still glad."
- Except in large groups, if more than one person checks in, it is recommended that all do so.
- HAPPY may be substituted for GLAD, and SCARED may be substituted for AFRAID.

.

CELEBRATE CLOSING THE GAP

"Harry, Cedric, I suggest you both go up to bed," said Dumbledore, smiling at both of them. "I am sure Gryffindor and Hufflepuff are waiting to celebrate with you, and it would be a shame to deprive them of this excellent excuse to make a great deal of mess and noise."
- J.K. Rowling, Harry Potter and the Goblet of Fire

Closing the me-you gap isn't only about being more efficient and effective, or getting the job done, or being action-focused. It's about human life, and the joy that we have being with each other, saying "I love you" and showing people we care about them. It can be easy to let days go by without making our love and joy known to others.. It's important that we stop, often, and celebrate our connections.

Celebrate reaching milestones. Brag a little about the goals you've reached. Bake a cake, eat food together, hoist a tankard or clink your glasses. Sing, dance, do cartwheels, wave your arms in the air. Run in a field, play guitar, play bike polo, paint each other's faces. Have a campfire, play a game in the public square, make a human pyramid. Pat each other on the back. Thank each other. Smile at each other.

Celebrate your connections. Reinforce your humanity and playfulness and joy so you have enough energy and interest to continue when things are hard. And you can celebrate because you want to celebrate, nothing more. Do it for the joy of it. Integrating celebration, art, music, food, play and adventures into your work makes the strands of the web you're creating together stronger and easier to repair if they ever break.

I've worked with a company that has a culture of focusing on failures and ignoring successes. They rehash the mistakes and missteps of the past over and over, ostensibly to avoid the same mistakes in future. But when something goes well, when someone has a great idea and executes flawlessly, when a team has a breakthrough or a customer shares their delight with the service they've experienced, it's treated as a footnote, almost a mistake in itself, in the daily grind of fire fighting and drama.

The problem is, in their drive to weed out the failures, they are reinforcing failure by focusing exclusively on it. Their great work, wins, successes and innovations get much less attention than their work to keep the drama and pain alive. So what do people work on? Talking about and fighting over what's not working well to the exclusion of doing more of what's right. Take a lesson from them, and include celebration and reflection on what's working well in your work to generate optimism and energy for what's coming next.

Achievement of Personal Alignment evidence is a great focus for celebration. I have set evidence for my Personal Alignment and then "forgotten" about it. Months later I find my alignment notes and discover that I've actually achieved several of the things that were a challenge to me when I set them in writing. Looking back on my achievement I realize what was once a struggle is now a skill in my toolkit. I always have a little celebration to mark my achievement.

When I wrote down my first Personal Alignment evidence in 2003, I made several commitments to myself: I said that in five years I would be living in a house on a hill with a view and water, and that the house would be filled with art we had made; I said I would have paid for my half of that house with money I had made by sharing my ideas; I said that I would have written a book.

Now, many years later I live in that house with Paul. It sits on a hill, with a view, and there's a lake down the road. Paintings we have made hang on the walls. I have been sharing my ideas and being paid for it. And this is my second book. Paul and I celebrate our achievements often, to have fun together, and to reinforce what we want to continue to do in our lives. Our celebration could take the form of a special meal together, a walk on the beach, or just a simple conversation to share how happy we are.

Paul and I were BootCamp Instructors when we met Yves Hanoulle at his first McCarthy BootCamp in the fall of 2005. At the time he and his girlfriend Els were not yet married. As he worked on his Personal Alignment and his evidence at camp, I had the privilege of Investigating him. We had some great, sometimes tearful, talks about his relationship and his dream of one day getting married to Els, and he decided to include getting married in his long-term evidence.

Yves and Els were married on May 25, 2012. In my wedding congratulations to Yves, I reminded him of his long-term evidence and our conversations years ago. He had not consciously remembered that he had made that commitment to himself at BootCamp, and yet, he fulfilled it.

And so, as a special celebration of Personal Alignment evidence achieved, I would like to offer this chapter to Yves and Els as a wedding present, celebrating the power of intention, of Personal Alignment, and a beautiful example of using the Core to close the me-you gap.

MASTER CLOSING THE GAP

When we try to pick out anything by itself, we find it hitched to everything else in the Universe.
- John Muir

GO DEEPER, GET CLOSER

*Action has meaning only in relationship and without understanding
relationship, action on any level will only breed conflict. The understanding of
relationship is infinitely more important than the search for any plan of
action.*
- Jiddu Krishnamurti

We've been learning and practicing, and the good news is this is just the start.
Masters never stop learning and practicing. They keep their "chops", or skills,
up. They show up to the tennis court, the piano, the batting cage, and the
keyboard every day, even if they'd rather stay in bed with a cup of coffee.

Every day, masters practice their serve for the 10,000th time, or practice
every scale twenty times, or hit fifty baseballs, or write two thousand lines of
code. Then, when they've practiced again, masters take the rules and tools
they know intimately and play with them. They combine the rules and tools in
new ways, turn them upside down, and combine genres, styles and disciplines,
just to see what will happen. They do things "experts" say shouldn't work just
to see if the theory is correct. They learn.

So this chapter is about keeping your chops up with the tools to close the
gap. I've said that if each of us learns these tools, closes the me-you gap with
one person, and then each of us moves on to the next me-you gap, soon the
me-you and the us-them gaps will be closing up everywhere. So this is about
making closing the gap a personal practice that will be a model for the world.

I love watching the folks who master closing the gap. They don't put a
limit on who they'll Ask For Help, or why. They make connections
everywhere they go and show that safety in vulnerability is a smart, effective
choice.

People who go deep in their Check Ins inspire me too, sharing themselves
and modeling vulnerability and creating a paradoxical strength that brings

trust. And there are those who ask for Perfection Game on anything they think of, including how to do the dishes, how to order dinner at a restaurant, and how to talk to the boss. The masters just get out there with their Core toolkit and try stuff.

Master practice is deliberately asking for help, or investigating someone, or checking in every day. Being engaged and present with your kids or partner every day. Working toward the evidence you created for your Personal Alignment every day. Making only decisions that align with that evidence. Passing or checking out or saying no every single time you don't want to do something. Yep. There's no back door or day off if you want to master this stuff. Every day brings a new chance to learn, to play and to model closing the gap.

Adding more intensity is another way to work your chops. Check in about things that you don't want others to know about you. Tell people your secrets. The first secret you tell will be the hardest. It'll leave you sweating and looking over your shoulder. Then the next one will be easier, and soon there won't be any secrets to spend time and energy hiding from others and you can use your newfound energy to play.

To Investigate more intensely, ask the lurking questions, the questions you're not sure they want to answer, and you're not sure you want them to, either. They're the questions you're both stepping over. The ones that are keeping you apart because they're taking up the space between you.

Another way to Investigate intensely is to ask only "What" questions. "What happens when you do that?" "What is the most important thing you could do now?" What would be different if this were a good thing instead of a bad thing in your mind?" "What is your favourite restaurant?" "What would make this perfect for you?" "What do you love to do when you have free time?"

In fact, when you want to ask a question, say the word, "What" and then fill in the rest. I guarantee you'll soon be asking the kind of curious, open-ended questions that create the greatest connection.

Ask people for help who you're not sure want to help you. Ask that weird guy in the other department. Ask the woman who runs the post office. Ask a stranger. Ask your mother, your kids, the love of your life.

Who are the scary people in your life? Family, experts, heroes, critics, enemies? Ask them for help and see what happens. Investigate them and ask for their ideas. Ask them to perfect your ideas. Check In with them. Notice trust expanding in your life, like bread rising.

When we master something we can become so good at it that we use it unconsciously. We use the essence of it without using the form. That's an ideal situation. If we can get so good at meeting the Core Commitments that we are living them every day unconsciously, we are truly mastering the basic fundamentals of closing the me-you gap.

LOST IN THE WOODS

> If you see a whole thing - it seems that it's always beautiful. Planets, lives....
> But close up a world's all dirt and rocks. And day to day, life's a hard job, you
> get tired, you lose the pattern.
> - Ursula K. Le Guin

What happens if we forget to practice? Days go by and we don't Check In, we forget our alignment and our commitments. We lose our place, misunderstand each other, and begin pulling back to our side of the me-you gap.

That's the time to pull out the Core toolkit and go back to the basics.

Here are some possibilities for getting back on the road if you find yourself in the weeds:

Old Habits

Doing what we've always done

Using tools we're unfamiliar with feels uncomfortable. Just like our New Year's resolutions, when the thrill of novelty wears off, it's easy to shrug off the Commitments and use only the Protocols that are familiar. We tell ourselves our customers or colleagues won't get it, our families think we're weird, rules are for other people, and just for today we're going to have a day off, promising ourselves that we'll try them again tomorrow when we have more time. We get into arguments and forget we can Check Out. We struggle with something for hours and forget we can Ask For Help. We get lonely and stay lonely because we think that's just who we are and how the world works. We let the gap slide open between us, like a door we forgot to close.

When it feels hard, Ask For Help. When you think you're the only one who cares, Ask For Help. When you feel lonely, Ask For Help. Got the idea? *Try this Simple Tool:* Ask for Help

Doing what the boss says

Authority figures are lightning rods for our deepest fears: fear of being abandoned, of being punished, of not being loved. We project these fears onto the boss and do dumb things on purpose.

You know your idea will work but the boss tells you to do something you know will be a disaster. Instead of sharing your concerns with the boss you shake your head and criticize the boss, complain about the company and retreat into helplessness.

It's exactly the same thing we did with our parents when we were teenagers. We were told what to do, we hated it, and we believed we had no choice. The complaining was our stress relief.

But we're grown up, skilful and smart now. We have lots of choices. And if we want to live in a world of choice and trust, we need to support the best idea even if it's our own. You can say "Boss, I realize this is your decision, and you're in charge, but I'm afraid your idea has some flaws that may make us both look bad, and I have an idea that may help,"

The boss will thank you. And if she doesn't, do you really want to work there?

Follow this Simple Rule: Never do anything dumb on purpose

Scarcity thinking

Humans live in a world we've created that evolved as we responded to the signals from the limbic region of our brains. It governs the fight, flight, or freeze response. It kept us alive for millions of years. And it lives on in our work and lives together. We can easily slip back into the world of not enough time, money or people.

But when we practice and become skilful with the tools for closing the me-you gap, we can replace those fight or flight responses. We can think and feel at the same time. We can, instead, create a reality in which we have abundant time, help, love, support, ideas, and opportunity. All the help we need is available to us all the time.

Follow this Simple Rule: Use the Core Protocols or better.

Silos:

Silos happen when me-you gaps turn into us-them gaps.

I create silos when I say, "I'll only talk to the people with the same interests I have," or, "I won't talk to anyone from Sales," or, "there's no point in asking for help from the intern; what could he know that I don't?" Or, "Those people are different. I'm going to stay with the people I know."

Silos start are in our minds. I make the choice whether or not to talk to people who aren't "technical" or who are "new to the company" or who work in a different country, region, office, or department.

Age, gender, experience, skill, length of time with the organization; all of these are potential boundaries between us. The us-them gap is the me-you gap multiplied many times. Us-them has the same solution as me-you. Connect with people one-to-one.

It's not just people on my own team with whom I need to close the gap. It's people on other teams, in other regions, with other experience. Only when I Ask For Help beyond the boundaries of what is comfortable for me will I have access to the infinite range of value, connection and help that is just waiting for me to connect with it.

Try this Simple Tool: Ask For Help

Kumbaya

Nice vs. honest

When we get close, supportive, generous of spirit and trusting, we can become fearful of losing access to those feelings by voting against the crowd, behaving differently, leaving the room, or working on something by ourselves. We let conflict go unresolved and pussyfoot around each other so we don't hurt feelings. This usually leads to a kind of anxious paralysis. No one wants to say what needs to be said for fear of making others uncomfortable, or shaking up the friendly atmosphere.

Nice vs. honest actually kills trust, slowly and insidiously. When I hold back my true thoughts about the product we're working on, or your behaviour, or about how I'm feeling, it's the beginning of an endemic culture of lying to be "nice."

Being the first person to shake up Kumbaya is uncomfortable, but never as uncomfortable as the moment, months or years from now, when there's no other option, and we both have to admit we've been lying all along.

Follow this Simple Rule: Know and disclose what you want, think, and feel.

Not wanting to be apart

When we don't use the Core Commitments and Protocols to close the me-you gaps we live in isolation from each other. We tend to stay apart by choice because working together is intensely frustrating and soul-numbing.

When we've first adopted the Core and committed to each other, our delight in being with each other can make us reluctant to work apart. We want to be everywhere at once, everywhere our team is working. But sometimes it's more productive for us to leave.

Follow this Simple Rule: Disengage from less productive situations.

Tired of being together

In the honeymoon phase of being together I may also be reluctant to admit I don't want to participate in the team's activities. This is true of couples, too. I agree to every event, every game, every activity, because I can't bear to be apart from the people who are so fascinating to me.

But eventually I get tired, I realize there are things I'm not interested in, I have family to go home to or I just want a break. But by this point, I feel strange being odd-man-out.

The very best thing for both of us is for you or I to Pass or Check Out as soon as we know we want to. If you need to go do something more important, I should support you. When I want to Pass or Check Out, I will, knowing you'll support me. Freedom and safety are integral to the Core. Without freedom to choose where and who we want to be and safety from reprisal, the trust we've created together is just a sham.

So go ahead and Pass on that game or Check Out when you need to go for a run. I will thank you for it.

Try these Simple Tools: Pass, Check Out

Holding back

Zombie

I've checked out without physically leaving. I'm half awake, and not even half present. You notice it. My energy is dragging you down. My apathy and disinterest is creating a kind of black hole that's swallowing the energy of everyone in the room. The gap will start to open up if I hang around you and others while I'm really unwilling or unable to contribute or share. When I've become a zombie I need to Check Out and physically leave.

Try this Simple Tool: Check Out

Lies

When people lie, they kill intimacy. There's just no excuse for lying when you're on a team using the Core. You know that everyone has everything they need to look after themselves, so there's no need to keep a difficult truth from someone. And if you know and disclose what you want, think and feel, there's no reason to withhold truth about your intentions. Have integrity, and insist on it with others. When you want to know if someone's telling the truth, ask. There is no other way of knowing.

The hardest part is starting with you. To never, ever lie is a challenge, especially if you've worked in an organization at which lying is accepted. We lie to the boss if we know something he or she won't like.

For instance if a project is going to be late or cost more than estimated, most people choose to lie. And the lie at the end is because of the lie at the beginning, when we pretended to know how long the project would take, or the lie in the middle, when we realized things weren't working out the way we expected and we planned to just "make up the time" later.

Lies on teams are like lies between spouses or partners. A small lie becomes a bigger lie, and soon the foundation of trust has become very brittle. The team grieves for the loss of trust, and then adjusts by adopting lying as its inevitable mode of operation.

Paul and I worked with an organization once that institutionalized keeping bad news from executives. The story the staff told themselves and us was that the executives would be upset if they told the truth. It was agreed the executives were being unreasonable.

When Paul and I suggested telling the executives the truth about the dysfunction in the organization, the staff politely advised us that the executives would never stand for hearing what we had to say, and they had to change our message so the executives would accept it. We argued for some time with the staff about the message, but in the end, the message the staff wanted to deliver was the one they believed the executives wanted to hear, and we weren't invited back. A few years later the organization went bankrupt, after a series of irregularities caused shareholders to abandon the stock because they didn't trust the governance of the company. Was misrepresentation endemic in the company? Perhaps.

Lying doesn't just affect the me-you gaps we are part of. We become slaves to keeping the lie alive with every conversation we have across all the me you gaps we want to close. Our tolerance of a "harmless" lie now may become a multi-armed network of lies later, just like the ones that have plagued our financial systems. Lies are costly to maintain and stressful to discover. We have enough costs and stress already. Let's replace systemic lies with systemic integrity, one truth at a time, and one gap at a time.

Try these Simple Tools: Intention Check, Protocol Check

Autopilot

Discussion

Talking without proposing a decision with action is a waste of time unless the talking is getting us closer to the best idea. Talking without proposing is what the majority of our time together at work constitutes. We get together in big rooms and talk. And talk. Meetings are scheduled for hours at a time. And is anything accomplished in that time except to review what we talked about last time? There's a common misperception that talking means communicating.

But talking can be grandstanding, arguing, persuading, marketing, justifying, whining, complaining, stonewalling, or entertaining. It isn't necessarily getting a decision or us closer to trust. Usually if we've been talking for more than ten minutes without someone proposing action, we're probably talking as a substitute for closing the me-you gap.

This happens a lot in many organizations. We get together in meetings to get human contact, because we spend so much time on computers that we miss being with others.

But instead of seeking real connection by investigating, asking for help, working on ideas, or sharing ourselves, we sit and talk about things we don't care about. Sometimes we believe we are bonding because we're all so frustrated together. We need to stop, and, as one friend says, "close the gab."

If you're in a meeting, listen for the best idea on the table and make a proposal. Use the Decider Protocol and resolve with Resolver to stop unnecessary babble. Then when the Decider is accepted, start working on the idea right away with anyone who wants to help.

Finally, make a plan to get the group together for some social time to reconnect, using the Protocols to connect deeply, and to celebrate getting something done.

Try this Simple Tool: Decider

Boredom

Boredom usually comes from monotony. When you have been doing the same activity for a long time, with the same people, using the same information, and your thinking has narrowed to a small, predictable model, you'll probably be bored.

Go find some new me-you gaps to close!

Ask the janitor for help. Find a landscape architect and ask him about his life and what he finds exciting in his work. Investigate the clerk at the driver's license office about his hobbies. Talk to the woman who runs the homeless shelter.

It's almost unimportant what you ask. What is important is that you don't limit your choices to what you already know and are comfortable with. Invite new selves into your space for just a few moments.

For some of us, talking to new people like this can be a bit (or a lot) unnerving. But remember, we have safety gear for just this moment. We can Pass, Check Out and say No. We have a virtue that can help us stay focused on what we want so we don't go down a rabbit hole. We can experiment. So give some new conversations a try and see what happens.

A hidden source of great conversations is the people with whom you do business. Your dentist, the check-out clerk at the grocery store, and the waiter. These are the people who are around you all the time, with whom you usually talk only about the transaction you're currently conducting.

But what would happen if you were genuinely curious about them and asked about them and their world? Or asked them for help with a problem you're working on? People who do business through transactions with people often can see things about you that you are blind to, or have insights into human nature that could help solve a wicked problem in your life.

For others of us, those who are comfortable talking to lots of new people, boredom might come from the shallowness of our conversations. So instead of adding more people to your conversation list, how about having deeper conversations with the people you already know?

And how about your partner or spouse? When was the last time you didn't assume you already knew the answer, but instead just asked him or her "What's exciting to you? What's fun, interesting, scary, worrying? If you could ask me anything what would you ask? What's on your "bucket list"? What would make our relationship 10/10 for you?"

Parents, kids, siblings, neighbors, and old friends can all be a great source of fascinating new information if you just put aside your assumptions and ask questions as if you didn't know them at all.

Dig a little. If Uncle Harry tells the same old story over and over, why not ask him about the details? What did he feel and think about the experience? Was it scary? Did it change him in some way? If he could do it all over again, what would he do?

Try these Simple Tools: Investigate, Ask For Help

Drama

Scapegoating

Every group has at least one scapegoat. It's the person on the team who becomes the excuse for the team's mediocrity.

The person could be young, old, shy, flamboyant, senior, junior, casual, formal, technical, artistic, logical, emotional, articulate, halting. However the team has typecast him or her as an obstacle to moving forward. Whatever characteristic the scapegoat has becomes a lightning rod for the team's drama.

Team members spend time talking about how "that person" is getting in their way. She might talk too much, or not enough. He might be too aggressive or too accommodating. He might work too hard, or not work hard enough. The team, one person at a time, uses difference between that person and the rest of the group to distract themselves from change, growth, learning and challenge.

If you catch yourself scapegoating someone, intentionally learn about him. Look below the shallow description you've assigned to him. Our peripheral vision opens up when we seek to perceive, and we move beyond simplistic black and white thinking to see the whole person and all of their complex motivations and facets.

Closing the me-you gap by learning more about each other is the antidote to typecasting, segregation and pigeonholing. Investigate him. Ask her for help. Ask him to perfect your idea. Ask her what her alignment is and how it's working out.

Try these Simple Tools: Investigate, Ask For Help

Pacifying/ rescuing/ persecuting

Useful conflict can be resolved, but dramatic conflict continues on and on, apparently with a life of its own. When drama takes over, you may feel the urge to pacify the angry person to make the conflict go away. But unless there is physical danger involved, often the best approach is simply to ignore the drama. If you can't resolve the argument, or if the other person appears to want to continue arguing, just leave and take care of yourself.

Let your Personal Alignment guide your choice when you want to move away from unending drama. Think about what you want, the evidence you want to use your virtue to achieve, and go get it.

Working on your own goals and achievements will keep you away from the conflict or drama long enough to get some mental and emotional space, to let the drama die down and for you to assess whether or not to return and try to resolve the outstanding disagreement, or to just let it go.

Try this Simple Tool: Personal Alignment

Arguing

Arguing is a failure to resolve a disagreement.

We both have to agree to seek resolution if we want the argument to stop. Prolonging an argument is an attempt to keep the drama alive.

Drama is addictive because it feels energetic and fascinating. After all we pay money to watch people argue on TV, in movie theatres and on stage. When it's right in front of us – and we don't have to pay money for it – it's hard to pull ourselves away.

While we don't pay money out of our wallets to observe or contribute to drama in our lives, we do pay a price. Our relationships suffer from constant confusion and uncertainty, and we become physically and emotionally drained. Leave drama to the actors, and instead seek to engage in only rational and coherent conversations that result in resolution and peace.

We both have to agree to find excitement elsewhere, and use Resolution to get there. Ask what it would take for your partner to resolve the argument. If you are more emotionally invested in being right than in resolving the argument, Check Out and get what you need to come back ready to resolve the argument. Take your time, and consider self-care and help from others as key to your time away. Come back when you are feeling rational and prepared to end the argument.

Try these Simple Tools: Resolver, Check Out

Jealousy

When I have been doing my "duty" and working on only what I believe will make others happy, I get jealous of others who are getting what they want. But when I am getting what I want, I never feel that. So, I need to know what I want, and go get it. In fact, I need to want to help myself as much as I want to help others.

Try this Simple Tool: Personal Alignment

MAKE SOMETHING TOGETHER

Skill to do comes of doing.
- Ralph Waldo Emerson

We test our principles, and ourselves, when we create together. Armchair philosophy often can't stand up to real work. It's also a way of practicing, field testing the tools, and finding new ways of adapting and combining them for your own use. So let's make something together.

"What should we make? Who decides?"

We do. Once we're aligned in our thinking, who else could decide better? When we can close those gaps between us, and have rational, useful rules and tools as our common language, any product is within our reach.

You're a leader, then I, then you are, then I am. The best leader is the person with the best idea who can get others to help her make that idea reality. And anyone can have the next best idea.

Hierarchical position, seniority, race, age, gender, ethnic background, language, religion, region, education; none of those matter. Everyone has the potential to share the killer idea to make our work more elegant, useful, effective, or attractive.

Also, don't worry about having the right surroundings, meeting rooms, ambiance or games, except to support closing the me-you gaps. People want to connect in their own way, time, and place. They want the freedom to choose when to work together and when to work apart, when to share ideas and feelings and when to be silent, and where to work. Help make that freedom possible.

I don't have to know what you're doing or be in your presence all the time once we trust each other. We can work apart, or together, in different ways, at different times and using different tools. When we have closed the gaps, you and I, and by extension each of our teams, will be able to align our products quickly and easily. With the simple rules and tools of the Core Protocols and Commitments at their foundation, the me-you gaps in even large organizations become easy to close and culture becomes an asset rather than a hindrance.

KEEP AND CHECK PROMISES

Promises are the uniquely human way of ordering the future, making it predictable and reliable to the extent that this is humanly possible.
- Hannah Arendt

"He missed the deadline *again*!"

"What did you say to him last time?"

"I didn't say anything. I wanted to see if he would come to me and apologize. Obviously he didn't. I just can't trust him."

Promises are tests of trustworthiness and how we make and keep promises is a measure of mastery of closing the me-you gap.

There are three steps to a promise:

1. The agreement
2. Fulfilling the agreement
3. Consequences

When we say "yes" to an Ask For Help, we have made a promise. Trust starts with being honest about your commitment to fulfill the agreement. If you ask me to walk your dog this afternoon, I need to tell you honestly if I'm willing to walk your dog. Because once I've said yes, you're expecting me to walk the furry critter. If I go skydiving instead, then I'm off the trust list.

So I have to know what I want (is this sounding like a broken record yet? Getting the hint that Personal Alignment is pretty important?) and I have to tell you what I want. But what if I really want to get on your good side? I want you to like me. Or I want to do you a favor so you'll do me a favor in future? Or you're my boss and I want to do you a favor so you'll promote me sooner. Or I'm in love with you and want you to think I'm a nice person so you'll go out for dinner with me.

Stop the presses! Let's slow this right down. We're trying to close the me-you gap, right? We're talking about building trust. Hidden agendas and playing games are great for spy novels, and maybe there's a lot of that going on in our daily lives.

But hidden agendas are what make the gap *bigger*, not smaller. And the more complicated our motives, the harder it is to know what we really want and disclose that to others. So let's tease out the promises from the motives.

You asked me to walk your dog. Do I want to? No, because if I promise to walk it, then I can't go skydiving. What's more important to me? Well, skydiving. So I'm going to say no. Because I'm not willing to make a promise and then break it. At least if I tell you no now you can find someone else to walk little Frisky. Or I could help you find someone if I want to help.

Behaving in this kind of rational way let's you in on a lot of information about me: I don't make promises I won't keep, I like skydiving enough to not break a fixed appointment, and I'll tell you the truth about me. All of those things are much more valuable for closing the me-you gap than if I didn't do what I wanted, kept it to myself, resented missing my fun, and then broke my promise to walk the dog because I think I can get away with it.

Let's take a work example. You're the boss. You ask the team and I to work on a project. You ask me to give you an estimate of when it will be finished so I can tell the board of directors and the customer.

I have no idea when it will be finished because we've never done this kind of work before, but I've taken lots of certifications and estimating how long things take is what you pay me to do.

I know the estimate is always wrong and we can never know how long something new is going to take, but you're paying me a lot of money, so I spend a week or so and put together a presentation with milestone dates, costs and numbers of people we need. You take that to the board and the customer. And we never deliver on a single estimated date.

Is this different from promising to walk the dog knowing I won't?

Don't promise something you know you won't deliver. That means knowing what you won't deliver and practicing fierce integrity. It might mean making some hard decisions about the kind of work you do or how you do it. But if you want to close the me-you gap, if you want trust, you have to make only promises you can keep, and to reveal that you can't keep a promise as soon as you know you can't.

Now on the other side, you as the boss, are really upset. The team kept missing deadlines, over and over. You want to fire them all! But you never confronted them about the missed promises because you're uncomfortable putting people on the spot like that. Why can't people be as responsible as you are? Why can't they just tell the truth?

But then you realize that you've been covering up the missed deadlines when you go to the Board and to the Customer. You realize that after the very first failure to meet a promise you should have asked the team what happened and what would be different next time.

And you owed it to the Board and the Customer to tell them the truth; the team wasn't going to deliver what was promised. The customer is angry not just because the team failed, but because the boss lied about progress.

What a mess. Can you hear the voices echoing down the canyons of the me-you gaps all over this organization? The vultures are circling overhead.

So, before we ever get here, we're going to ask people about missed promises; promises about walking the dog, delivering on time, doing what we said we'd do. And we're going to assume there was good intent, intent to do what was promised, but that there's some obstacle in the way. The conversation can be about that obstacle, what the people making the promise are doing about it, and what will be different next time.

That conversation itself, an honest one about a missed promise and what will be done about it, is a powerful way to close the gap.

CONCLUSION

Today the network of relationships linking the human race to itself and to the
rest of the biosphere is so complex that all aspects affect all others to an
extraordinary degree.
- Murray Gell-Mann

Though we are living in a time of increasing public sharing and
transparency, the tools we use to do it are holding us back. We have to
negotiate every conversation, decision, and promise.

It reminds me of the early days of automobiles. Before there were rules of
the road, car drivers had to negotiate every intersection with every other
driver who showed up at the same time. These negotiations often descended
into shouting matches, and even fist fights, in the street over who had the
right of way.

It seems to me that as we take advantage of new tools for interaction and
collaboration, we are like those drivers. We have the machine for moving fast,
but without an agreement about structure, we are recreating the same rules
over and over again. In spite of the blazing speed of our interactions, we're
getting stuck at the intersections.

We have an opportunity to make our work, and our day-to-day lives, less
complicated. We can make more time to be with people we care about in a
meaningful way, do work that matters to our loved ones, and us and enjoy
one another and our world. The time we need is right in front of us, and it
starts with closing the me-you gap.

I can't do it alone. None of us can. But someone has to go first.

Let it be us.

OTHER RESOURCES

My previous book, Creating Time, is a introductory team handbook on using the Core for creating time on teams. It's available on Amazon and Kindle.

The Core Commitments and Protocols (The Core) are continually evolving as our world evolves. For the most current version of The Core, more resources, more protocols, and other supporting information, see http://liveingreatness.com/core-protocols/

The Booted is an ongoing online extension of BootCamp. To join the group, search for The Booted in Facebook, and ask to join. We'd love to close the gap with you.

The Core is the result of observing great teams in a lab, called BootCamp. BootCamp is an opportunity to learn the Core in an intensive, challenging, business simulation. Paul Reeves and I offer BootCamps and coaching in your location for your team. Please contact us at Vickie@simplerulesandtools.com to learn more.

Software For Your Head is the original book on the Core, by Jim and Michele McCarthy. You can get a copy at www.liveingreatness.com or at their own website, www.mccarthyshow.com. Their website also has a wealth of information about the Core, including podcasts, articles and blogs.

BIBLIOGRAPHY

All chapter title quotes from http://www.wisdomquotes.com and http://www.goodreads.com/quotes

Csikszentmihalyi, Mihaly. Finding Flow the Psychology of Engagement with Everyday Life. New York: Basic, 2008.

Eoyang, Glenda H. Coping with Chaos: Seven Simple Tools. Cheyenne, WY: Lagumo, 1997.

___HSD Professional Certification Training Content, Cohort 15, Ottawa, Canada, Fall, 2010.

___"Conditions For Self-Organizing In Human Systems", The Union Institute and University, 2001

McCarthy, Jim, and Michele McCarthy. Software for Your Head: Core Protocols for Creating and Maintaining Shared Vision. Boston: Addison-Wesley, 2002.

Nancy, Kline. More Time to Think: A Way of Being in the World. Fisher King, 2010.

Page, Scott E. The Difference: How the Power of Diversity Creates Better Groups, Firms, Schools, and Societies. Princeton: Princeton UP, 2007.

Wheatley, Margaret J. Leadership and the New Science: Discovering Order in a Chaotic World. San Francisco: Berrett-Koehler, 1999.

Wheatley, Margaret J. Turning to One Another: Simple Conversations to Restore Hope to the Future. San Francisco, CA: Berrett-Koehler, 2009.

BIOGRAPHY OF THE AUTHOR

With her beloved partner, Paul Reeves, Vickie Gray coaches business leaders, and instructs team workshops that help people learn how to create time and close the me-you gap so they can live the lives they want.

With Paul, she lives in Nova Scotia, Canada, with two clever, retired greyhounds and a flock of wandering chickens.

Her previous book, Creating Time, is about using the Core to create time on teams.

You can find her on Twitter or Facebook as adaptivecoach.

Her website and blog are www.simplerulesandtools.com.

To contact her directly, email Vickie@simplerulesandtools.com

1650749R00060

Printed in Germany
by Amazon Distribution
GmbH, Leipzig